How to double your profits within the year

John Fenton is one of the leading experts on industrial selling
in the UK. After founding the Institution of Sales Engineers in
1965, he played a major part in the formation of the Institute
of Sales Management and the Institute of Purchasing Management. Over a number of years, his experience as a consultant
and trainer has given him close involvement with well over
20,000 practitioners of the arts of buying and selling. His
own management role as Chairman and Managing Director of
the Sales Augmentation International Group combines
with his training and consultancy experience to make
him a unique and outstanding figure in sales and
marketing in the UK. He has published two other
books: *The A-Z of Sales Management* (available in Pan)
and *The A-Z of Industrial Salesmanship*.

Also by John Fenton
in Pan Books

The A-Z of Sales Management

John Fenton

How to double your profits within the year

An action plan for your business

Pan Books
in association with Heinemann

First published 1981 by Pan Books Ltd,
Cavaye Place, London SW10 9PG
in association with William Heinemann Ltd
4th printing 1983
© John Fenton 1981
ISBN 0 330 26321 8
Printed and bound in Great Britain by
Cox & Wyman Ltd, Reading

Contents

This is a Different Kind of Book

It has four objectives:
1. To improve your attitude towards Profit.
2. To prove to you that it is **EASY** to double your current profit margin, and more.
3. To show you HOW to do it.
4. To provide you with all the tools you will need to have it actually happen back at your own business.

To achieve this fourth objective, this book has been constructed in the form of an example Action Plan for profit improvement, issued by the group managing director of Universal Widget Corporation to all his group senior executives.

If you can put yourself in the shoes of Universal Widget's GMD, you should be able to rewrite this example Action Plan to suit your own needs.

If you are in the position of one of Universal Widget's senior executives, you should be able to achieve for yourself some of the profit improvements contained within this document. Alternatively, you could bring it—and the whole concept—to the attention of your own GMD. Or, of course, you could do both.

Whichever—good profiteering!

John Fenton

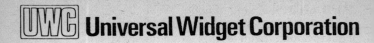

UWC Universal Widget Corporation

From the Group Managing Director
To all Senior Executives

Subject: PROFIT—an Action Plan for radical improvement

This Action Plan will require your individed attention and your total co-operation. Don't bury it in your pending tray; read it NOW. Take it home and read it in bed. Take it with you to the loo. Think about it while you shave and shower.

This is probably the most important document ever to have emerged from my office.

Be ready to discuss everything in detail at next month's group management meeting. The entire agenda will be devoted to this one subject.

Contributions and suggestions to be circulated well in advance, as usual, please.

GMD

PAST AND PRESENT

Recently, our auditors delivered our detailed results for the last financial year. Profits were average for our kind of industry. None of our divisions suffered serious problems. Our new products and new divisions are all doing fine; well on the way to break-even and on, or ahead of, schedule.

The Chairman's report indicates that all divisions expect to maintain steady progress for the foreseeable future, and all our budgets have been prepared accordingly.

Things are looking pretty good.

Also recently, we were visited, each division in turn by a management consultant retained by me personally to take a short, sharp, critical look at our business and advise me of anything that struck him as deserving more or better attention.

Okay, I know what most of you have been thinking, so I'll say it first. Why bring in a management consultant when the business is doing so well?

My reasoning was that if there ARE ways to improve our business which we ourselves haven't come up with yet, then I'd rather know NOW, while things are doing well, because there is more money available to do something about it than there would be at a time when things were less rosy.

Another reason is because we—the executives running this business—are often far too close to the action to be able to see the wood for the trees. I don't mean that derogatorily. I'm as big a duffer as the next man when it comes to falling into the "too-close-to-the-action" trap.

None of us have anything like enough of what I will call "thinking time"—the few minutes every day when we should take two paces sideways and try to look critically and impersonally at our respective parts of the business.

I say "try" in all seriousness, because most of us fail. And we fail because we are each of us too personally involved doing our thing to achieve that all important "separation".

A management consultant doesn't have this personal attachment to a particular piece of the action. He comes in with a completely open mind, conditioned only by the know-how he has acquired from business situations, good and bad, which he has observed and helped to improve in hundreds

3

of other client companies. Accepting the confidentiality of all this know-how—we are still bound to benefit from it.

He doesn't get side-tracked from asking embarrassing questions about how we do the job—questions we rarely ask ourselves. Questions which seem to begin..... "Why.....?"

He doesn't get bogged down and blinkered with the traditions and habitual practices of our business, so he asks questions about the things we DON'T do—questions we again rarely ask ourselves. Questions which seem to begin..... "Why not.....?"

I think you will all agree that I picked a management consultant who pulled no punches at all. I know quite a few of you were tempted to throw him out on his ear while he was with you; but you didn't, and I thank you for your patience, or tolerance, or whatever it was held you back.

In any event, the proof of the pudding, they say, is in the eating, and what our management consultant has done for Universal Widget Corporation you see before you now—in the form of this Action Plan.

You be the judge.

FUTURE

Every Action Plan has to have an Objective. Here is ours:-

WE ARE GOING TO DOUBLE OUR PROFITS WITHIN THE YEAR, OVER AND ABOVE THE PROFIT TARGETS IN OUR MAIN BUDGETS.

We are going to do this irrespective of what our markets or our competitors may be doing during the year. We are going to achieve this objective with very little additional revenue or capital expenditure over and above our existing budgets, and with no increase to our current work force, sales force or other human resources.

We are going to DOUBLE OUR PROFITS by implementing—and making work—some of the recommendations made by our management consultant. Only some. Apart from those in this Action Plan, there are many more which I have designated as lower priorities. These we will tackle next year.

Now before you go overboard with incredulity at the thought of doubling profits in one year, when all we have ever looked for in the past is a steady ten percent in a good year, let me say that I, too, scoffed more than a little when our management consultant suggested that a 100% improvement could easily be achieved.

Therefore, I think it only fair that I show YOU how it can be done, in the same way our management consultant showed me.

Profit

There are only three fundamental ways to increase profit:-

1. Reduce the fixed costs (overheads) and the variable costs of our business.
2. Raise the selling prices of our products and services (or lower the discounts).
3. Increase the sales turnover.

Reducing costs comes a logical first because money saved is better than money earned. (This should be obvious. If it isn't—think about it until it does become obvious.)

If we consider the structure of Universal Widget's manufacturing divisions in much simplified money terms, then for every £100 of sales turnover, £50 is spent on making the products (the variable costs of the materials and direct labour), £40 is spent on fixed costs (the overheads) and £10 is left as gross margin—the profit before tax.

In our distribution divisions, the structure is somewhat different. Here, for every £100 of sales turnover, £70 is spent on buying in the products we sell (the variable costs), £20 is spent on fixed costs (the overheads) and again £10 is left as gross margin—the profit before tax.

This is pretty near the norm for manufacturing and distribution throughout the world. And, of course, as the sales turnover increases, so the variable costs increase in proportion, but the fixed costs (the overheads) remain more or less stable, unless the increase in sales is pretty large.

That's the theory anyway, because every time OUR sales turnover goes up, our fixed costs seem to go up in proportion, along with our variable costs. And when we find a way to reduce costs, instead of this saving being reflected in our bottom line gross margin, we often seem to grow increasing

5

costs which absorb the saving somewhere else in the business, so that we gain nothing on the bottom line.

And whenever we raise prices or reduce discounts, instead of this being reflected straight down to the bottom line, we seem to find sales turnover reduced—the sales force blaming the higher prices, of course.

All too frequently, we seem to be robbing Peter to pay Paul. Our management consultant says it shouldn't be like that, and I must admit I tend to agree with him.

We should be able to apply some "treatment" to sections of our business and gain improvements WITHOUT the treatment adversely affecting other sections of the business and negating all the effort.

Shouldn't we.....?

Maybe we've been applying the wrong treatment to the wrong sections.

If you're still with me, let's now look at how much treatment—or rather how LITTLE treatment—it should take to achieve that 100% profit improvement.

If I set you a target, for example, of achieving just a ONE PERCENT improvement over the next twelve months in those three fundamental areas—reducing costs, raising prices and increasing sales—would you be confident that you could achieve these improvements without any adverse reactions from other parts of your operation?

Of course you would. Any competent excutive can improve his business by a mere ONE PERCENT given a year to do it in with his eyes shut.

But do you realise what those three ONE PERCENT improvements would do to our bottom line gross margin? I didn't and I bet you don't either.

So I want you to calculate just what a ONE PERCENT improvement of the three fundamentals does for our PROFIT figures. I want you to determine how much our gross margin will be improved if we could reduce our variable and fixed costs by one percent, raise our prices or cut our discounts by one percent, and increase our sales turnover by one percent, all at the same time, and WITHOUT any of this improvement having any adverse effects on the rest of the business.

Okay everyone. Get your calculators out. Here are two sets of Universal Widget "money boxes" to help you. One for the manufacturing divisions, and one for the distribution divisions. But remember, you are doing a COMPOUND calculation, from box 1, to box 2, to box 3, to box 4.

Fill in the numbers and see what you get for the box 4 gross margins. And please don't cheat and turn over two pages before you've got your answers.

Manufacturing

1 STARTING SITUATION

SALES	VARIABLE COSTS (Costs of making the stuff)	
100		50
	FIXED COSTS (Overheads)	40
	GM	10

2 COSTS reduced by 1%

SALES	VARIABLE COSTS	
	FIXED COSTS	
	GM	

3 PRICES raised by 1%

SALES	VARIABLE COSTS	
	FIXED COSTS	
	GM	

4 SALES increased by 1%

SALES	VARIABLE COSTS	
	FIXED COSTS	
	GM	

Distribution

1 STARTING SITUATION

SALES	VARIABLE COSTS (Costs of buying the stuff)	
100		70
	FIXED COSTS (Overheads)	20
	GM	10

2 COSTS reduced by 1%

SALES	VARIABLE COSTS	
	FIXED COSTS	
	GM	

3 PRICES raised by 1%

SALES	VARIABLE COSTS	
	FIXED COSTS	
	GM	

4 SALES increased by 1%

SALES	VARIABLE COSTS	
	FIXED COSTS	
	GM	

Here are the correct answers:-

(Just to cheer you up, your GMD got it all
wrong first time round.)

Manufacturing

1 STARTING SITUATION

SALES	VARIABLE COSTS (Costs of making the stuff)	
100		**50**
	FIXED COSTS (Overheads)	**40**
	GM	**10**

2 COSTS reduced by 1%

SALES	VARIABLE COSTS	
100		**49·5**
	FIXED COSTS	**39·6**
	GM	**10·9**

3 PRICES raised by 1%

SALES	VARIABLE COSTS	
101		**49·5**
	FIXED COSTS	**39·6**
	GM	**11·9**

4 SALES increased by 1%

SALES	VARIABLE COSTS	
102		**50**
	FIXED COSTS	**39·6**
	GM	**12·4**

Distribution

1 STARTING SITUATION

SALES	VARIABLE COSTS (Costs of buying the stuff)	
100		**70**
	FIXED COSTS (Overheads)	**20**
	GM	**10**

2 COSTS reduced by 1%

SALES	VARIABLE COSTS	
100		**69·3**
	FIXED COSTS	**19·8**
	GM	**10·9**

3 PRICES raised by 1%

SALES	VARIABLE COSTS	
101		**69·3**
	FIXED COSTS	**19·8**
	GM	**11·9**

4 SALES increased by 1%

SALES	VARIABLE COSTS	
102		**70**
	FIXED COSTS	**19·8**
	GM	**12·2**

So in our kind of business, if we can find a way to reduce costs by ONE PERCENT, raise prices by ONE PERCENT and increase sales by ONE PERCENT, without any adverse effects, we increase our profit in cash terms by 24 PERCENT for our manufacturing divisions and 22 PERCENT for our distribution divisions.

I have tried, and failed, to find a flaw in these calculations. If **YOU** find one, phone my office immediately.

(You can ignore the question of returns on capital invested; they're irrelevant to what we are trying to achieve.)

If you accept the logic behind this set of calculations, you also have to accept, as I had to, that to DOUBLE our profits, all we have to do is find a mere dozen hitherto unseen problems within our group to which we can apply the ONE PERCENT IMPROVEMENT WITH NO ADVERSE SIDE EFFECTS treatment.

And that, as I hope we have already agreed, we can all do with our eyes shut.

There are many combinations we can pick from. Here, for example, is a 100 PERCENT profit improvement for the manufacturing divisions, in cash terms, based on a FIVE PERCENT reduction in costs, a THREE PERCENT raise in prices or cut in discounts, and a FIVE PERCENT increase in sales; and a 100 PERCENT profit improvement for the distribution divisions in cash terms, based on a FOUR PERCENT reduction in costs, a TWO PERCENT raise in prices or cut in discounts, and a THIRTEEN PERCENT increase in sales.

Manufacturing

1 STARTING SITUATION

SALES	VARIABLE COSTS (Costs of making the stuff)	
100		**50**
	FIXED COSTS (Overheads)	**40**
	GM	**10**

2 COSTS reduced by 5%

SALES	VARIABLE COSTS	
100		**47·5**
	FIXED COSTS	**38**
	GM	**14·5**

3 PRICES raised by 3%

SALES	VARIABLE COSTS	
103		**47·5**
	FIXED COSTS	**38**
	GM	**17·5**

4 SALES increased by 5%

SALES	VARIABLE COSTS	
108		**50**
	FIXED COSTS	**38**
	GM	**20**

Distribution

1 STARTING SITUATION

SALES	VARIABLE COSTS (Costs of buying the stuff)	
100		**70**
	FIXED COSTS (Overheads)	**20**
	GM	**10**

2 COSTS reduced by 4%

SALES	VARIABLE COSTS	
100		**67·2**
	FIXED COSTS	**19·2**
	GM	**13·6**

3 PRICES raised by 2%

SALES	VARIABLE COSTS	
102		**67·2**
	FIXED COSTS	**19·2**
	GM	**15·6**

4 SALES increased by 13%

SALES	VARIABLE COSTS	
115·3		**76·1**
	FIXED COSTS	**19·2**
	GM	**20**

If you're now almost as convinced as I am, we can move on to some of the potential treatment areas which our management consultant pin-pointed during his time with us.

This Action Plan contains more potential treatment areas than any of you need in order to make that 100 PERCENT profit improvement target, so each of you should be able to pick a few favourites and leave out a few nasties (until next year).

All the treatment areas in this Action Plan, can in my opinion and our management consultant's, yield at least a ONE PERCENT improvement in one or more of the three fundamental areas during the next twelve months. From some we should achieve much more, and as you go through the Plan, I want you to estimate for yourself, for each treatment area, the percentage improvement you reckon **YOU** can achieve and write this down in the 'ratings' box provided with each treatment area.

Then, when you have reached the very end, add up all the percentages you have estimated for reducing variable costs, reducing fixed costs, raising prices, cutting discounts and increasing sales, and with these totals calculate the compound profit improvement you will achieve if you fulfil all your estimates, using the set of Universal Widget money boxes provided right at the end.

I shall be interested to see, next month, how many executives succeed in TREBLING our profit targets, let alone doubling them.

It takes all the running you can do to stay in the same place.

Lewis Carroll
Through the Looking Glass

TREATMENT AREAS
FOR
REDUCING
COSTS

1–THE DEBTOR–CREDITOR SITUATION

How long does it take to screw up our Cash Flow?

How much does it **really** cost us when it happens?

What happens to our Debtor situation when the Credit Controller goes on holiday—or falls sick?

Are our salesmen on the ball when it comes to getting the money in faster?

Do our salesmen agree terms of payment with customers **BEFORE** they accept the orders?

Do they really care whether we get paid or not?

Are our buyers on the ball when it comes to maximising on supplier credit?

A recent Government survey revealed that 70,000 British firms have no form of credit control whatsoever.

We are **NOT** one of those 70,000 firms, but we certainly need to pull our socks up.

What answer did you give to the first of the above questions —How long does it take to screw up our Cash Flow?

3 months?   6 months?   1 month?

Okay, so consider this example:-

One of our distribution divisions has a turnover of £1 million per year. That's £20,000 turnover per week in round figures.

On average, the customers of this division take 5 weeks to pay our sales invoices. So this division needs to finance 5 x £20,000 worth of Debtors at any one time.

i.e.   £100,000

It doesn't have to find all this £100,000, of course, because it gets some credit from its suppliers to set against this financing requirement.

The suppliers—Creditors—account for 70% of the sales turnover, and the division takes an average of 6 weeks credit before paying its bills.

Thus, it gains 6 x £14,000 = £84,000 at any one time, from its Creditors.

So the division only has to find £100,000 less £84,000, i.e. £16,000 from its cash resources, other parts of the group, or the bank, to stay in business.

BUT WHAT HAPPENS WHEN A NATIONAL SHORTAGE OF SUPPLIES COINCIDES WITH THE CREDIT CONTROLLER GOING SICK?

The Creditors demand payment in 4 weeks or they threaten to cut off supplies; and the Debtors are allowed to drift to 6 weeks average because there is no one around to keep his finger on the "pay-up" button.

So instead of £84,000 being funded by the Creditors, this drops to £56,000. And instead of £100,000 being required to finance the Debtors, this increases to £120,000.

And the money required to keep the business going rises from £16,000 to £64,000—IN ONE WEEK.

Here's a real life example from a company very like our own in make-up and the way it goes about its business, but with different figures:-

The company's annual sales turnover, as shown in its end of year accounts, was £23,310,300. Its annual amount spent on purchases (a figure obtained from the company's accountants) was £12,386,820 for the same year.

The end of year Debtor situation was shown from the end of year accounts to be £4,741,585. Likewise, the end of year Creditors situation was £1,741,000.

From these four figures, the company could work out its average weeks credit allowed on sales, and its average weeks credit taken on purchases, using the following formulae:-

Average Credit Allowed on Sales

$$\frac{\text{DEBTORS}}{\text{SALES}} \qquad x \qquad 52 \text{ weeks}$$

Average Credit Taken on Purchases

$$\frac{CREDITORS}{PURCHASES} \quad \text{x} \quad 52 \text{ weeks}$$

Thus the company calculated—

Average Credit Allowed on Sales

$$\frac{£4,741,585}{£23,310,300} \quad \text{x} \quad 52 \quad = \quad 10.6 \text{ weeks}$$

Average Credit Taken on Purchases

$$\frac{£1,741,000}{£12,386,820} \quad \text{x} \quad 52 \quad = \quad 7.3 \text{ weeks}$$

Not happy with the imbalance of this situation, the company determined to reduce the Credit Allowed on Sales to 8 weeks and take a bit more Credit on Purchases, to bring this also to 8 weeks.

Working the sums back from this 8 weeks target, this is what the company found—

Reduced Credit Allowed on Sales (RC)

$$\frac{£3,586,200 \text{ (RC)}}{£23,310,300} \quad \text{x} \quad 52 \quad = \quad 8 \text{ weeks}$$

Therefore Extra Cash generated = £4,741,585 − £3,586,200

= £1,155,385

Increased Credit Taken on Purchases (IC)

$$\frac{£1,905,664 \text{ (IC)}}{£12,386,820} \quad \text{x} \quad 52 \quad = \quad 8 \text{ weeks}$$

Therefore Extra Cash not spent = £1,905,664 − £1,741,000

= £164,664

Thus, the TOTAL CASH GENERATED FROM THIS EXERCISE WAS

£1,155,385 + £164,664 = £1,320,049

Pleased the Bank no end!

I don't need to tell you what to do—or what the answers to those other six questions at the beginning of this Treatment Area should be, do I?

1–THE DEBTOR–CREDITOR SITUATION

Your personal estimate of the percentage improvement possible.

Prices	Variable Costs
Sales	Fixed Costs (5%)

The figure in brackets is our management consultant's estimate of the probable percentage improvement in a business where this specific treatment area is a major problem.

Use this space for notes and calculations.

2–ANALYSING CUSTOMERS FOR PROFIT CONTRIBUTION

Two of our divisions supply consumable items to a wide range of industrial customers on a regular basis. Thus, for these two divisions, one of the highest costs is physical distribution.

Our analysis of customers in these two divisions has up till now been on a "number of orders" related to "sales turnover" basis. Our Management consultant suggests that this kind of analysis is not enough, and advises additional analysis to show % contribution to profit as well as sales, so as to highlight the effects of distribution costs.

The following example from another regular consumable supplier to industry will be pretty close to the figures our two divisions should come up with:-

Size of Customer by Average Monthly Purchase	No. of Customers as a percentage of total Customers	% Contribution to total sales	% Contribution to total profit
Less than £40	35%	16%	2%
£41 to £100	40%	38%	8%
£101 to £200	20%	30%	50%
£201 and above	5%	16%	40%

Once this analysis had been done, it was easy for this particular firm to see that 90% of its total profit contribution came from the 25% of customers that placed more than £101 worth of orders per month. From this it became very easy to point the salesforce in the right direction, and also to re-jig physical distribution and delivery patterns.

Comparisons between different sizes of order can be extremely valuable. Here is another example, this time for a paint manufacturer that wanted to establish the economics of

23

selling 20 tins per order as against 100 tins per order. Over 100 customers that placed 20 tin or 100 tin orders, this is what the paint manufacturer found:-

Transport   Transport costs for a 20 tin order were 82% of the transport costs for a 100 tin order.

Packing   Packing costs for a 20 tin order were 84% of the packing costs for a 100 tin order.

Invoicing   Invoicing costs for a 20 tin order were 89% of the invoicing costs for a 100 tin order.

Selling   Selling costs for a 20 tin order were 98% of the selling costs for a 100 tin order.

Bad Payers   The cost of chasing bad payers for a 20 tin order were 108% of the costs of chasing bad payers for a 100 tin order.

Profit   A 20 tin order gave a net profit on turnover of 0.5%. A 100 tin order gave a net profit on turnover of 4%.

No prizes for guessing which way this company went. Or what **YOU** need to do.

2–ANALYSING CUSTOMERS FOR PROFIT
Your personal estimate of the percentage improvement possible.

Prices	Variable Costs (5%)
Sales	Fixed Costs (5%)

The figures in brackets are our management consultant's estimate of the probable percentage improvement in a business where this specific treatment area is a major problem.

Use this space for notes and calculations.

The obscure we see eventually,
the completely apparent
takes longer.

3–MINIMISING DELIVERY COSTS

Why do our consumables divisions deliver three times a week?

Is it because our customers **DEMAND** deliveries three times a week? Or is it because our competitors deliver three times a week? Or is it because we've **ALWAYS** delivered three times a week?

This ties in closely with my previous treatment area headed "Analysing Customers for Profit Contribution".

I have been told of a supplier of replacement windscreens in Australia who used to deliver three times a week to its garage and windscreen fitting customers. The supplier's marketing manager decided that such frequent deliveries were both uneconomical and unnecessary. So he instructed his distribution centres to change delivery programmes so as to provide a **TWICE A WEEK** delivery service.

Three months later, he found that for half his distribution centres, the delivery programme change had been a complete success—with all customers happily accepting the twice-a-week deliveries and physical distribution costs down by 20%.

But he found the **OTHER** half of his distribution centres were experiencing considerable difficulties. Well over half of **their** customers were complaining bitterly about the reduced service. The competitors were having a field day and employee morale was low and getting lower.

The marketing manager couldn't understand it. The problem was not geographical, because the successful distribution centres were often next to the unsuccessful ones in their strategic positions across Australia. Successful centres could be urban or rural, in housing estates, commercial areas, industrialised areas or the bush. So could unsuccessful centres.

Thus, it had to be in the centres themselves, not the customers, where the problem lay. And it took the marketing manager another three months to find it, and to be sure.

The key was in how the staff in the distribution centres

27

spoke to their customers about the change of delivery programmes. The successful centres, when they received telephoned orders for replacement windscreens, said to the customers:

"Our next delivery in your area will be Wednesday. Will that be okay?"

95% of the customers said "Yes—that's okay". For the remaining 5% who could not wait, special arrangements could often be made, including having an employee of the centre deliver the windscreens on his way home from work.

The unsuccessful centres, when **THEY** received telephoned orders for windscreens, said more:

"We've recently had to reduce our deliveries from three times a week to twice a week, due to economies. So we can't get the screens to you until Wednesday. Will that be okay?"

75% of the customers said "No—that's **not** okay!" They felt they were getting inferior service and automatically objected to it.

If the staff of the centre hadn't **TOLD** them it was now twice a week when before it had been three times a week, no problems would have been encountered.

Such is the thin line between success and failure.

Look at your delivery programmes. See what improvements you can make. But be sure to write the scripts of your office and telesales staff so that you don't fall into the same trap as our Australian windscreen supplier.

3–MINIMISING DELIVERY COSTS
Your personal estimate of the percentage improvement possible.

Prices	Variable Costs
Sales	Fixed Costs (5%)

The figure in brackets is our management consultant's estimate of the probable percentage improvement in a business where this specific treatment area is a major problem.

Use this space for notes and calculations.

4–RECRUITING THE RIGHT PEOPLE

Only the very best Head Hunters in the executive recruitment business can guarantee a success rate of more than 50%. This means that, on average, out of every 10 people taken on, only five turn out to be the round pegs required for the round holes.

Down the line towards the shop floor the average success rate is even lower. This doesn't necessarily mean that more than half the people we recruit leave us within six months and are replaced. It could be worse than that. It could be that the majority of our people are classified as "barely acceptable"—in other words "totally unsuitable for additional responsibility" or "cannot work without regular supervision"—but not so bad as to deserve being fired.

I don't need to tell you how much it costs to recruit and train a new employee, executive level or shop floor level. A hell of a lot of money, and increasing steadily. The cost to us of employing square pegs in round holes must be even greater.

Thus, it behoves us all to consider much more closely how we go about interviewing and selecting the people we take on, and how the executives below us do likewise.

Why do do many good managers make bad interviewers? Not because the techniques are difficult, but because they think they don't need them. They are privately confident that they know a good man when they see one, and that's that.

There are four principal faults which occur time and time again.

1. Failure to prepare properly for the interview.
2. Failure to banish any interruptions whilst the interview is proceeding.
3. Failure to draw the interviewee out and get him talking freely.
4. Failure to ask direct, probing and sometimes blunt questions.

Incredible though it may seem, many interviewers fail on 3 and 4 because they don't want to risk hurting the interviewee's feelings!

We do no training whatsoever in the techniques of interviewing potential employees. We should. I am advised by our management consultant that a good starting point is for us all to see a half-hour training film titled "Man-Hunt" and available from Video Arts Ltd., Dumbarton House, 68 Oxford Street, London WIN 9LA.

So during next month's meeting, we will be seeing this film.

If we can improve our performance in this area, there will be really big and long term cost savings and also improvements in the sales turnover in respect of any sales personnel involved. In this respect, link this section with my subsequent section headed "Performance Appraisal".

However, there are a few other things to consider, well before we even begin to tackle interviews of prospective new bodies.

Every time the business finds itself with a sudden hole, because someone has quit, been fired, been promoted, been moved sideways, transferred, retired, left to have a baby, taken a sabbatical to get a degree or to sail single handed round the world, gone to the funny farm, been thrown in jail, taken hostage, shot or just died, we have an opportunity to re-assess the whole situation and re-organise a few things if it aids efficiency.

Thus, we may find we don't need another body, or we need a different kind of body to the one we just lost.

Then we have the job specification to draft, and from this the man profile. (This applies equally to woman, of course).

Only then are we ready to start looking for bodies—drafting advertisements, selecting appropriate media, briefing employment bureaus or head hunters.

We also need to have prepared a draft service contract and to have a clear idea of pay, terms, conditions, holidays, pension, company car, and anything that is part of the 'remunerative package,' and what the theorists like to call 'the hygiene elements'.

Finally, if we have time to plan the recruitment of staff

properly (and with sudden holes time isn't usually on our side) we must take account of the total costs of the whole recruitment operation and the time it takes for any new recruit to become profitable to the company.

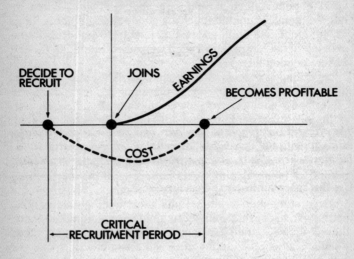

Consider the graph. Money is vertical: time, as usual, is horizontal. From the point in time at which the decision to recruit is made, money is being spent. By the time the new body joins the company, costs are pretty high. They keep increasing thereon in until the new body starts earning his keep. But the new body is not truly profitable until all the costs have been re-couped, including the costs of training him and paying him. Thus, we may be faced with a nine months 'critical recruitment period' to cover in our cost budgets, three months to find a body, and six months to make him show a profit.

And if we get the **wrong** body, we write everything off, stay in after school and do it all over again.

4—RECRUITING THE RIGHT PEOPLE

Your personal estimates of the percentage improvement possible.

Prices	Variable Costs
	(10%)
Sales	Fixed Costs
(10%)	(10%)

The figures in brackets are our management consultant's estimate of the probable percentage improvements in a business where this specific treatment area is a major problem.

Use this space for notes and calculations.

5–PARKINSON'S LAW

The cost of a business executive is one of the largest items on any company's overhead. It follows that to reduce the number of executives in any business can provide the greatest possible savings, assuming of course that the reduction does not impair business efficiency.

This has to be questionable. We all do important and highly contributive jobs in this organisation. So do our subordinates and their subordinates. Take any executive away and the gap is bound to result in chaos.

Our management consultant has other ideas, and in fact can speak from first hand experience, having had the unenviable task of reducing the number of senior executives and administrative staff in a number of organisations because "Parkinson's Law" had taken its insidious hold. He has, therefore, seen the effects of such action on these organisations and measured, on a "before and after" basis, morale, business efficiency and the costs of running the business.

A reduction in executive staff of 5 in one organisation actually increased business efficiency and output, radically improved morale and saved more than £100,000 in the first year.

He uses as a back-up the originator of "Parkinson's Law" to add weight to his ideas, asking me a straight question — "Have I ever read C. Northcote Parkinson's famous book, first published in 1958 by John Murray?" I had to admit that I had not. Now I ask you the same question—"Have you read Parkinson's Law?" If you haven't, then get hold of a copy and read it before next month's meeting. It's still in print.

Let C. Northcote Parkinson himself explain—

1. "EXECUTIVES WANT TO MULTIPLY SUBORD-INATES, NOT RIVALS.
2. "EXECUTIVES MAKE WORK FOR EACH OTHER".

1. Picture an executive called A, who finds himself over-worked is real or imaginary is immaterial, but we should observe, in passing, that A's sensation, or illusion, might easily result from his own decreasing energy; a normal symptom of middle age.

   For this real or imagined overwork there are, broadly speaking, three possible remedies.
   (i)   He may resign
   (ii) He may ask to halve the work with a colleague called B.
   (iii) He may demand the assistance of two sub-ordinates to be called C and D.

   There is probably no instance in history of A choosing any but the third remedy. By resignation he would lose his pension rights. By having B appointed, on his own level in the hierarchy, he would bring in a rival for promotion to W's job when W (at long last) retires. So A would rather have C and D, junior people, below him. They will add to his consequence and, and by dividing the work between C and D, he will have the merit of being the only man who comprehends them both.

   It is essential to realize at this point that C and D are, as it were, inseparable. To appoint C alone would have been impossible. Why? Because C, if by himself, would divide the work with A and so assume almost the equal status that has been refused in the first instance to B: a status the more emphasized if C is A's only possible successor.

   Subordinates must thus number two or more, each being kept in order by fear of the other's promotion.

   When C complains in turn of being overworked (as he certainly will) A will, with the concurrence of C, advise the appointment of two assistants to help C. But he can then avert internal friction only by advising the appointment of two more assistants to help D, whose position is much the same.

   With the recruitment of E, F, G and H, the promotion of A is now practically certain.

2. Seven people are now doing what one executive did before. This is where factor two comes into operation. For these seven make so much work for each other that all are fully occupied and A is actually working harder than ever.

An incoming document or report may well come before each of them in turn. E decided that it falls within the province of F, who places a draft reply before C, who amends it drastically before consulting D, who asks G to deal with it. But G goes sick at this point, handing the file over to H, who drafts a note that is signed by D and returned to C, who revises his draft accordingly and lays the new version before A.

What does A do? He would have every excuse for signing the thing unread, for he has many other matters on his mind. Knowing now that he is to succeed W next year, he has to decide whether C or D should succeed to his own job. He was concerned that G suddenly went sick. He is worried whether H will soon go likewise. He has looked pale recently—partly but not solely because of his domestic troubles.

Then there is the business of F's special increase in salary for his period at London Office and E's application for transfer to Scotland. A has heard that D is in love with a married typist and that G and F are no longer on speaking terms—no one seems to know why.

So A might be tempted to sign C's draft and have done with it. But A is a conscientious man. Beset as he is with problems created by his colleagues for themselves and for him—created by the mere fact of these colleagues' existence—he is not the man to shirk his duty.

He reads through the draft with care, deletes the fussy paragraphs added by C and H, and restores the thing to the form preferred in the first instance by the able (if quarrelsome) F. He corrects the English—none of these people can write grammatically—and finally produces the same reply he would have written if officials C, D, E, F, G and H had never been born.

Far more people have taken far longer to produce the same result. No one has been idle. All have done their best. And it is late in the evening before A finally quits his office and journeys home, reflecting with bowed shoulders and wry smile that late hours, like grey hairs, are among the penalties of success.

C.N.P

The frightening reality of this famous piece of 1958 prose must come home to all of us. I am not advising you to fire half of your administrative staff. Of course not. But I am certainly asking you to be aware of what Parkinson's Law tells us.

Examine your working procedures. Cut out any duplication of the same tasks. Make sure that in your part of the organisation Parkinson's Law is minimised. You'll never banish it completely, no one has ever done that, but being aware that it exists is half the battle. Knowing how to recognise it is the other half.

Be even more ruthless if you feel you need to be, because our management consultant has pin-pointed a number of places where he feels Parkinson's Law is getting too strong a hold. I would rather you found these places and dealt effectively with the situation yourself before I get to talk to you more specifically about it.

5—PARKINSON'S LAW
Your personal estimate of the percentage improvement possible.

Prices	Variable Costs
Sales	Fixed Costs (40%)

The figure in brackets is our management consultant's proven result in a business where rampant "Parkinson's Law" was ruthlessly minimised, a £240,000 fixed cost overhead being reduced by £100,000 with no loss of operating efficiency.

Use this space for notes, calculations or for drafting your resignation.

At some time in the life cycle
of virtually every organization,
its ability to succeed
in spite of itself runs out.

6–THE COMPUTER

"DEAR CUSTOMER,

I AM THE UNIVERSAL WIDGET CORPORATION COMPUTER.
PART OF MY JOB IS TO DRAW YOUR ATTENTION TO THE
OVERDUE BALANCE ON THE ATTACHED STATEMENT.

SO FAR, ONLY YOU AND I KNOW THAT THIS BALANCE
IS OVERDUE, BUT IN SEVEN DAYS TIME I AM
PROGRAMMED TO TELL THE CREDIT CONTROLLER.

WHY SHOULD WE INVOLVE HIM ?"

If you like this little message as much as I do, it will probably be coming home to you that there are things we can do with our computer that we haven't even begun to think about—and probably more useful things than we are doing at present.

THE problem with the way we use our computer is not the old **GIGO** (Garbage In—Garbage Out) problem, more a sort of subconscious urge to generate more and more statistical data, which involves more and more people, and is steadily generating more and more resentment.

Why resentment? Because everyone except maybe our computer itself (or should it be himself or herself?) knows that we don't **USE** more than one fifth of the data we generate.

So stop it! Keep it simple, or if you want it in technical jargon—"simplicate and add lightness". Get your output down to the bare critical essentials and bugger the rest.

Stop thinking that your division is losing out because another division or department is using more computer time than you are. Maybe we should have bonuses for the people who use the computer **least**.

Then start thinking of how we can make our computer more human. Thinking this way will automatically separate the senseless statistics from the things that earn us money—and we'll all benefit and learn to love that sexy black box.

6—THE COMPUTER

Your personal estimate of the percentage improvement possible.

Prices	Variable Costs
Sales	Fixed Costs (10%)

The figure in brackets is our management consultant's estimate of the probable percentage improvement in a business where this specific treatment area is a major problem.

Use this space for notes and calculations.

7–PURCHASING POLICIES

We have too many old established buying habits.

Make note that 92% of all products in use in today's world have been introduced within the last ten years. And just as our salesmen spend too much of their time calling on old established customers who are easy to do business with, so our buyers spend too much of their time receiving the same small group of salesmen they prefer doing business with.

So very quickly indeed, our purchasing programmes become out of date and we fall behind when it comes to using the most efficient components and at the best possible prices.

A good buyer should make a point of seeing half a dozen **new** salesmen, from suppliers we do **not** do business with, every week. Only by doing this, and doing it systematically, will we be keeping on the ball. This also applies to our design and production staff who have a buying responsibility, and to our works engineering departments.

In cases where we buy on contract, our buyers should be inviting every reliable established supplier of the commodity or product involved, and every new supplier where little is currently known of performance, to bid for our contract each time it comes up for renewal.

Our buyers should be making sure we use the supplier's warehousing space, not our own, by calling off regular weekly or monthly requirements instead of accepting deliveries in bulk.

Each of our buyers is responsible on average for spending £1 million of our money. Do we appreciate this, or do we take it for granted? Do we give our buyers any on-going training? Do we send them on courses? Do we encourage them to **visit** suppliers and check them out first hand?

No we don't.

We don't even have any kind of directory to hand to

salesmen who visit our various divisions, telling them what kind of products we buy and which buyers are responsible for which products. Hasn't anyone realised how much time such a directory would save our buyers and receptionists, at how little cost?

Further—we don't have any formal specification for the way in which suppliers and potential suppliers quote for our requirements. So we receive quotations in all shapes and sizes, making it very difficult and time consuming for our buyers to compare like with like.

We should be getting our suppliers to do more of our chores for us. What our management consultant suggests for a start is that we issue the following instruction to all our suppliers, present and future, in respect of the way they quote us:

TO ALL SUPPLIERS

PROCEDURE FOR SUBMITTING QUOTATIONS TO UWC AND ITS SUBSIDIARIES

All quotations should give the following information in the sequence as listed. Quotations which do not follow this procedure will not be considered.

1. *Begin all quotations with a brief statement of the objectives we wish to achieve by having your equipment/products/services.*
2. *Follow this statement of objectives with a brief outline of your recommendations, and explain—briefly—how your recommendations fulfil our objectives.*
3. *Elaborate on 2, with a list of any additional benefits we will receive from your recommendations.*
4. *Explain with the full use of figures, finance, times, labour rates, maintenance costs, depreciation periods, production outputs, verifiable comparisons, whichever are relevant, how we can justify the purchase of the equipment/products/services or how we can justify changing from our present suppliers to you.*

   All prices must be inclusive, i.e. include delivery, installation, commissioning or whatever necessary.

   If the quotation is for supplies of products over a contract period, detail the options you can offer for regular call-offs so that we can achieve one of our objectives of minimising our stock levels without adversely affecting our production flow.

5. *State the Guarantees you provide. Give details of your after-sales service facilities and how they operate.*
6. *Give at least three names, addresses and telephone numbers of firms we can contact and with which you do business on the equipment/products/services concerned in your quotation. Preferably, firms situated near to us.*

Think about the ramifications of such a procedure being followed by all our suppliers. How much easier will it be for our buyers to assess competitive quotations and make the right decisions? What would this save us over a full year—not just in our buying administration costs are used?

Finally, our management consultant has pinpointed one more error in our buying ways. We leave it all too often till the last minute before placing orders with suppliers. Maybe because of pressure of work, maybe in the hope of a better deal coming up, maybe because our buyers are not sure.

The result of this last minute buying is that our suppliers let us down on delivery more often than they should, our production departments are held up more often than they should be, and our buyers spend far more time than they should chasing suppliers to try to get supplies faster.

It's a chicken and egg situation and, to a large extent, human nature is the prime fault.

See if you can improve on this problem in your own division. Here is a "funny" which you might be able to use to make the message stick.

RUSH JOBS CALENDAR

MIR	FRI	FRI	FRI	THU	WED	TUE
8	7	6	5	4	3	2
15	14	13	12	11	10	9
22	21	20	19	18	17	16
29	28	27	26	25	24	23
36	35	34	33	32	31	30

This is a special calendar which has been developed for handling rush jobs. All rush jobs are wanted yesterday, consequently all dates run backwards — with this calendar a client can order his work on the 7th and have it delivered on the 3rd.

Everyone wants his job by Friday, so there are three Fridays in every week.

There are five new days at the end of the month for those 'end-of-the-month' jobs.

There is no 1st of the month — so there cannot be late delivery of 'end-of-the-month' jobs.

No-one likes Mondays so these have been eliminated.

There are no Saturdays or Sundays, so overtime rates can be kept to a minimum.

There is a special day each week, Mirday, for the performance of Miracles.

7—PURCHASING POLICIES

Your personal estimate of the percentage improvement possible.

Prices	Variable Costs (5%)
Sales	Fixed Costs (2%)

The figures in brackets are our management consultant's estimate of the probable percentage improvement in a business where this specific treatment area is a major problem.

Use this space for notes and calculations.

8–STORES, STOCKS AND INVENTORIES

Stock, stock beautiful stock
Piles on the fixtures and more in the dock
Some of it ancient and some of it new
Alas, and tomorrow another lot's due

I am told that our stock levels right across our group are some 20% higher than they were this time last year. Okay, I know the supply situation has been more than erratic ever since the three-day-week, but just the same, our stock position gives cause for concern.

People have lost sight of the objective for Stocks. People have become used to taking precautions and, slowly but surely this has led to over-stocking.

It is costing us an arm and a leg, apart from what we are losing due to deterioration, breakage and thieving.

In an ideal world, we would have suppliers competing for our business and giving a first-class delivery. Raw materials would be in good supply. We would have standard, long-running production and we could cut stocks to practically nil.

But it isn't an ideal world. So stocks have to be held and stocks have to be controlled. There are, in fact, four main reasons for stock control:-

1. Materials and products required for manufacturing, sale or use by UWC must be available in the right quantity, at the right quality, and in the right condition, at the required time and place.
2. The level of stock needs to be kept as low as possible to keep capital investment in it to a minimum and avoid occupying excessive space with consequent high overheads.
3. The stock must be protected from deterioration, damage,

pilferage and indiscriminate wastage.

4. Information must be readily and accurately provided for financial control and for perpetual inventory checks which eliminate the need for costly annual stocktaking.

That's the theory. But it often breaks down in practice. Production all too often runs out of components or materials and grinds to a halt. Or our stores become half full of rusty castings which have kept coming in from suppliers in spite of the fact that we stopped using those particular castings months ago. Everyone blames the store keepers and stock control, the staff concerned take umbrage and things get worse rather than better.

The Human Element wins again—and everyone loses.

I've long wondered how this kind of problem can ever be completely resolved. All those thousands of components and products and lumps of raw materials. All those thousands of pieces of paper and card and dockets and computer print-outs that are supposed to keep tabs on all the stock. How can the human brain assimilate all that and successfully pin-point one shortage or one over-stocking situation, and take appropriate action whilst in the midst of the seething mass of requisitions, telephone calls, shouts of abuse, tea breaks, deliveries, call-off's and union meetings which beset every working day?

Frankly, it can't, and never could.

Our management consultant advises that, wherever possible, out stores layouts be changed to facilitate our stores personnel being able to check stock levels just by walking down each row of racking and using their eyes. No computer, no card index system, just eyes. Nothing, he claims, works anything like as effectively when it comes to making sure you don't run out of something.

The principle works from two key fundamentals:-

1. Stores racking should **never** be standardised. The racking should be designed for each item to be stored, i.e. Big boxes have big racks or pallets. Small bags have small racks or wiremesh bins. Tiny components have see-through plastic tubes rather than tote bins.

2. From the special design of racking in fundamental 1,

each pile of items is seen by the stores personnel as a **vertical** pile, which can be given a quantity scale like a thermometer. Three clearly visible marks are required on each item's scale—the highest mark denotes "Optimum stock level"; the middle mark denotes "Re-ordering level"; the lowest mark denotes "Emergency" level.

In a perfect world, all the stores personnel have to do once a day or once a week is police their stores, noting which items are due for re-ordering and for which items they need to ring the "Emergency" bells.

Okay, I know we do not work in a perfect world but there is a lot of common sense in what this principle tells us.

See what you can do about it.

8–STORES, STOCKS, INVENTORIES
Your personal estimate of the percentage improvement possible.

Prices	Variable Costs
	(5%)
Sales	**Fixed Costs**
(5%)	(5%)

The figures in brackets are our management consultant's estimate of the probable percentage improvement in a business where this specific treatment area is a major problem.

Use this space for notes and calculations.

9–ASSEMBLY EFFICIENCY

All our assembly lines suffer from one common fault. If one station runs out of a component, the whole line grinds to a halt until the rogue component is again available.

Ford Motors reckon every minute an assembly line is out of action it costs them well over £5,000. We aren't that high, but we're high enough.

I've been told of a method used by Carron Company, Falkirk, Scotland, on the electric and gas cooker assembly lines in its domestic appliance division, which minimises line hold-ups due to component shortages. It seems that the problem arises, not because station operators do not know when they are running short of anything, but because at the time they realise they are likely to run out of a component, they cannot find anyone in authority to tell, and they cannot leave their station, otherwise the line would grind to a halt anyway.

Okay, this makes the assembly line supervisors at fault—and likely they are. Carron have adopted a derivation of the 'sight' principle mentioned in the previous treatment area on Stores, Stocks and Inventories, to resolve the problem.

Each station operator has three plywood painted discs, about one foot diameter, which he or she can hang from a kind of gallows above the work station. The discs are coloured green, orange and red, just like traffic lights. A green disc hanging from the gallows means there is no danger of the station running out of any component for at least two hours. An orange disc means that the station will run out of something **within** two hours. A red disc means that the station will run out of something within half an hour.

The station operators fully understand what to do with these discs. And all the components at each work station are stacked or stored according to optimum/re-order/emergency levels.

The gallows are positioned so that the assembly line supervisor can see **ALL** the discs from any point in the shop. Thus, all **he** has to do is keep watch on the discs and get to any work station showing an orange disc—fast. "All Green" is his aim in life. More than a couple of reds and he's really in trouble.

The managing director of Carron's domestic appliance division considered installing emergency buttons at each work station, wired to a bell or a klaxon to back-up the red discs, but after consideration, decided not to. If he did this, he reasoned, the supervisors might sit in their offices until they heard the klaxon sound. Instead, he began making random visits to the assembly lines, and if he saw a red disc and there wasn't a good reason for it, heads rolled.

In a month, hold-ups had minimised and morale was much higher. The m/d kept it going by regularly showing visitors round the assembly lines and praising the way the operators worked the system. The operators loved it. It made them feel proud.

Diagrams

Another good suggestion for any of our assembly lines concerns the competence of our operators. Do they fully understand how our products should be put together? Which bit goes where—and which bit goes on first?

Meccano cracked this problem umpteen decades ago. Airfix and others followed on with their plastic construction kits. Now even the airline catering units use the idea when they make up those strange concoctions called "in-flight meals".

An exploded diagram (as on page 54) of how the thing goes together, numbered for sequence of which bit goes first, etc. Notes and instructions arrowed in as required.

Why not on our assembly work stations? An exploded diagram for each station, as large as possible, coloured as well. Even our most junior new recruit would have less problems with something like this to help fathom things out.

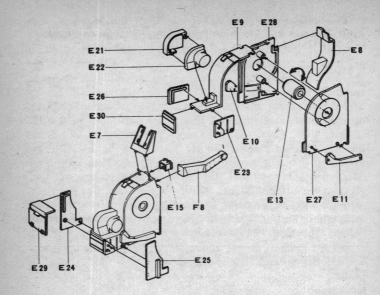

9—ASSEMBLY EFFICIENCY

Your personal estimate of the percentage improvement possible.

Prices	Variable Costs
	(5%)
Sales	Fixed Costs

The figures in brackets are our management consultant's estimate of the probable percentage improvement in a business where this specific treatment area is a major problem.

Use this space for notes and calculations.

10–PRODUCTION EFFICIENCY

In the short time he was with us, our management consultant pin-pointed at least a dozen areas where our efficiency in production could be improved and our costs likewise reduced. He only had time to go into detail on five of these dozen, one in our machine shops, two in our processes and two in our foundries. But the prodigious amount of money we can save from these five areas alone demonstrates the considerable potential for continuing examination in all our production departments.

Consequently, I am calling our management consultant back in a few weeks time for a more concentrated study of this specific treatment area, and the results of this study we will be dealing with separately from this present Action Plan.

One other point—at the beginning of this Action Plan I stated that the things we could do to improve Profit would only involve minimum additional expenditure. In four out of five of the examples following, expenditure on new capital equipment would be required in order to achieve our objective. However, all the equipment could be acquired on a lease/purchase basis over 3 to 5 years. In this way, the total acquisition costs would be fully covered by the savings we make in production, and still give us net savings from just about day one.

Machine Shops

We have two machine shops using a number of capstan, turret and centre lathes to machine steel and non-ferrous components.

These components are either used in our own products, or are machined by us for other companies on a sub-contract basis. Batch sizes vary from 10 to 1000 off per component. We've had our present machines for many years and we've several times considered automatics and numerical control, but vetoed change on the grounds of the batch sizes being too small and NC being too complicated on setting up to show sufficient benefits.

But we now appear to be somewhat out of date. We have not kept up with the speed of the last few years' developments in **Computerised** numerical controlled machines.

Equipment now available can be efficiently used for small batches like ours; tooling configurations can be set up on a machine to cope with a dozen or more different components without anything more than pushing a few buttons. Tape control is a thing of the past, it's all on the machine itself now, including a large capacity memory; metal removal is considerably faster; quality of surface finish is much superior; labour force required is reduced; labour force retained is much happier using the best and most up-to-date equipment.

There are quite a few good suppliers of this type of equipment. We took just one and conducted a quick survey of one small slice of our machine shops and the half-dozen components that slice produces. The supplier was the UK arm of a Swedish firm, SMT-Pullmax (GB) Ltd. The machine proposed is a Swedish built computerised numerically controlled lathe. We compared it against two of our existing machines, a manually operated turret lathe and a centre lathe, used exclusively to produce the six components. Thus, we have two existing machines and two operators compared with one new machine and one operator.

These are the production figures for the six components, projected across a full year during which a considerable amount of overtime is expected to be necessary to cope with demand.

Component	Quantity per year	Number of batches	One turret lathe, one centre lathe and two operators			One CNC Lathe and One Operator		
			Setting time Minutes per batch	Machining time Minutes per Component	TOTAL HOURS REQUIRED PER YEAR	Setting time Minutes per batch	Machining time Minutes per Component	TOTAL HOURS REQUIRED PER YEAR
1	1800	56	95	35	1139	52	12	409
2	2500	69	120	20	972	78	5	298
3	1500	100	75	45	1250	40	11	342
4	1200	43	60	28	603	28	8	180
5	2500	47	100	17	787	36	4	195
6	500	42	90	40	396	62	6	93
					5147			1517

Based on these figures, we estimate that such a CNC machine would not only effectively replace the the turret lathe and the centre lathe, but would also have sufficient capacity to also replace one other turret lathe. Thus, we would increase production speed and quality of components, whilst saving the costs of two operators and the space and running costs of two machines.

I don't want to get bogged down in fine detail in this Action Plan—the key objective is to make **YOU** think and act, not to do the job for you. So let me stop there on the subject of what we could do in our machine shops, except for the following article which appeared in the Journal of the Engineering Industries Association in September 1976, about a little sub-contract machining firm down in Dorset. How about this for setting an example?

NC and CNC in practice

We recently had occasion to visit a small sub-contracting company on the South Coast, and what we found there ably demonstrated what the average EIA member could do with NC and CNC equipment. The company, Binden Engineering of Wareham, Dorset, is run by two engineers, John Lawrence and John Rees. Formed in 1966 to handle jig and tool work, Binden quickly branched out into all kinds of production work.

Binden's introduction to NC came nearly four years ago, when John Lawrence bought a second hand SMT S10 NC lathe, not with any particular project in mind, but simply because Lawrence and Rees wanted to try NC and find out for themselves what it had to offer.

This attitude in itself would be looked upon as strange by the majority of engineering directors in Britain, and as utter madness by some, but perhaps it is this curiosity and determination to try something new that is lacking in much of British Industry today.

Binden found their secondhand S10 NC lathe so reliable (they haven't spent anything on it since it was installed) that Lawrence and Rees decided that NC had to be their future direction, especially as work was becoming harder to get and skilled labour very hard to find in Dorset. Four years ago, Binden had 40 employees, working centre lathes, turret lathes, capstans, millers, radial and pillar drills—and an output of around £80,000 a year.

Now the company has six NC and CNC machines, the labour force has reduced to 30 and output is up to £190,000, with £300,000 an easy target without further investment in plant or people.

The first NC lathe paid for itself inside 18 months and Binden bought a second SMT S10 NC machine at the end of 1973, brand new this time, on the strength of the performance of the first machine and the fact that the company had enough work coming in to fill its capacity. This second machine had paid for itself by the beginning of this year.

Any company experiencing this kind of success tends to standardise on make of machine, and Binden was no exception.

59

In January 1975 an SMT-PULLMAX Swedturn 15 CNC controlled lathe was purchased, with a significantly larger capacity than the S10 lathes. This enabled Binden to compete for larger turning work and screwcutting, which the CNC 220 system makes childsplay.

The transition from NC to CNC took SMT's engineer two days at Wareham, plus a couple of telephone calls to clear up queries. One secret of Binden's success is that John Lawrence has always made sure he is the first employee to learn to use a new machine and system. After that, motivating and training the labour force is simple.

Also in January 1975, Binden bought a Heller NC turret machining centre to cope with the milling, boring and tapping work generated from the NC and CNC lathe output. And in February this year, a fourth SMT lathe was purchased, this time a Swedturn 10 with CNC 220 control system. Strangely enough, this purchase was made at a time when work was radically falling off, but Lawrence and Rees knew that long term prospects indicated a firm future demand and they were determined to be in a position to compete with, and beat, their competition, when the up-turn arrived.

Latest acquisition is a secondhand Cincinnati NC controlled machining centre to increase the back-up to the lathe production, and handle efficiently and profitably a long running contract for gear box parts.

The future for Binden has to be rosy. Already few firms in the South can compete and, looking ahead, anyone would have great difficulty in catching up with Binden even if they were determined to.

The key factor in sub-contracting is pricing, and CNC has made John Lawrence's pricing tasks very much simpler. Binden is also spending far less money on tooling, mainly because so many different operations can be performed with the same tips, and tool life is much longer with NC and CNC. Surface finish with a good CNC system and the right lathe can consistently record down to 20 micro inches, which alleviates many grinding operations.

One particular job Binden used to tackle on a centre lathe normally took three weeks to machine the whole batch.

60

Switching the job to the SMT-PULLMAX Swedturn 15 lathe reduced the machining time for the same batch to two days for the first time this job was put on. Scrap is down from 5% to 1%, and John Lawrence summed up the entire success story with the comment:

'One component contract we tried to win, machined from 4½ inch diameter EN8 tube, we could never compete successfully for until we had the Swedturn 10 CNC lathe, mainly because of the complex screwcutting required. But with CNC and the ability to get down to 20 micro inches on the ST 10, this component can be finish turned in 12 minutes flat. I reckon we will have that contract for a long time to come'.

Wasting Water

We have a blind spot.

Everyone in UWC is fully aware of the need to conserve energy, and to the best of my knowledge, everyone is doing his best to make sure our energy costs are as low as they can be for optimum operating efficiency. But there is a source of energy for which we are charged which has been overlooked—and it costs us pretty near the same as electricity, gas and oil.

Water.

We use it in our processes, for cleaning, for dissolving, for diluting, and for cooling. And on cooling alone we can, I am told, save considerable sums of money if we stopped pouring our cooling water down the local sewer and re-processed it instead.

Okay, to do this we need to buy some plant, but the cost of the plant, as I've already said, would be amortised very quickly.

Look into your water costs, fast. The price we pay for water is likely to increase steadily, just like electricity, gas and oil.

Here are the results of a survey conducted by our management consultant of our principal process cooling situation:-

Situation: The company is using a lot of water to cool

production processes, the cooling water going to waste after being passed through the processes.

Proposal: To instal a cooling tower to cool the water after it has been used, and re-circulate it instead of allowing it to flow to waste.

Price of Cooling Tower and pipework for re-circulating: £9000

Calculations On Water Savings:

Rate of water flow—12,000 gallons per hour.

Amount of water used per day (8 hrs)   96,000 gallons
                          per week (5   dys)   480,000 gallons
                          per year (48 wks) 23,040,000 gallons

Cost of water used, at current charges of 30 pence per 1000 gallons, is £6,912 per year.

Company depreciates plant and equipment over 7 years.

Total cost of water used, over this 7 year period, assuming increases in water charges of 10% per year, would be:-

1st year	£ 6,912
2nd year	£ 7,603
3rd year	£ 8,353
4th year	£ 9,188
5th year	£10,107
6th year	£11,118
7th year	£12,230

Total Savings   £65,511 over 7 years
less cost of
Cooling Tower £ 9,000

Balance   £56,511

Amortization period: About 15 months

Maintenance of Process Valves

One of our process shops has around thirty ordinary ball valves, hand operated, for controlling the flow of liquids through all the pipework. The valves used are the same kind as we've used since the year dot. Our works engineers have about twenty in stock at any time, because on average each valve has to have its packing replaced once very two months, but the valves themselves are so cheap (about £5 each) that rather than fiddle about replacing packings, the engineers simply rip out the old valve and fit a new one.

At least it would be simple, were it not for the time it takes to change the valve—which is about two hours and involves two works engineers. That's two engineers for two hours for thirty valves for six times a year. That's 720 man hours a year. And 180 valves a year.

But much more important, that's 360 hours a year when part of our process is shut down and not producing.

Our management consultant has pointed out to me that there has been an alternate ball valve on the market for some years now which has a packing life of one year on average, and which can be serviced in 20 minutes, instead of 2 hours, and by one man. This valve is significantly more expensive, of course, and it is this fact which has deterred our works engineers from using it, they claim. (I suspect another reason might be that they see problems of using the major part of those 720 man hours in other, equally fruitful, directions.)

Such is the short sighted thinking of, I am sure, many of our employees. How we change these attitudes I am not sure, but on the question of these ball valves, change we can.

These are the figures produced so far on those thirty ball valves:-

	Existing Valves	New Valve
Cost of Valves per year	180 @ £5 = £900	30 @ £25 = £750
Man-hours per year on maintenance	180 x 2 x 2 = 720	30 x 20 mins = 10
At £5 per hour cost of works engineer, maintenance labour costs per year	720 x £5 = £3600	10 x £5 = £50
Average cost of loss of production during valve shut-down time £100 per hour. Thus, cost of loss of production per year	360 x £100 = £36,000	10 x £100 = £1000
Total Costs per year	£40,500	£1800

Doesn't it make you sweat?

_____

Building Sand Castles

We now move to our iron foundry, which is currently dumping about 350 tons of used moulding sand every week, at a cost of £3 per ton just to **DUMP** it. That's £1050 a week for building sand castles.

I can afford to jest, because this £1050 a week is but a drop in the ocean (or should I say a grain in the desert!). The fact is that our foundry, along with 80% of the rest of the foundries in this country and abroad, is guilty of throwing away these vast quantities of used moulding sand, whereas just about all of it could be reclaimed and used again, time after time.

This only applies to certain types of moulding sand, the resin-bonded air-setting varieties and the CO_2 varieties. We use resin-bonded sand, as do the majority of iron foundries, and on this I will concentrate.

Our management consultant has introduced me to a company in the Black Country, Foundry & Technical Liaison Ltd, that designs and builds equipment for re-claiming moulding sand. FTL has provided me with a set of costings which tell the whole story:

64

Our costs per week using sand only once and then dumping it:

350 tons of sand @ £12.50 per ton	£4,375.00
1.4% resin content = 4.9 tons @ £804 per ton	£3,940.00
Catalyst — 35% of resin = 1.71 tons @ £200 per ton	£ 342.00
Dumping used sand/resin acid 356.61 tons @ £3 per ton	£1,070.00
Total Costs per week	£9,727.00
Total Costs per 48 week working year.	£466,896.00

Our estimated Costs per week if we reclaimed our sand, using a FTL Fu-Reclaim sand reclamation unit (Operating costs £1.50 per ton of sand)

94% Reclaimed sand = 329 tons @ £1.50 per ton	£ 494.00
0.9% average resin = 3.15 tons @ £804 per ton	£2,533.00
35% average Catalyst = 1.1 tons @ £200 per ton	£ 220.00
6% new sand = 21 tons @ £12.50 per ton	£ 263.00
6% old sand dumped = 21 tons @ £3 per ton	£ 63.00
Total Costs per week	£3,573.00
Total estimated costs per 48 week year	£171,504.00
Estimated Costs saved in first full year	£295,392.00

Okay, here's the catch—the FTL equipment would cost around £100,000. But even then, this high capital cost is completely covered in 16 weeks—and that's without allowing for 100% first year Corporation Tax relief. If we were to buy the equipment on lease/purchase over 3 years, with no initial deposit, the repayments, at current interest rates, would be about £800 per week.

This still gives us savings of £5,354 per week, or £256,992 in the first full year. And with sand, resin and dumping costs likely to increase, it could be even more.

We couldn't use reclaimed sand for everything. Our cores would probably still have to be made from all new sand, or from something nearer and 80/20 mixture of reclaimed and new, but nevertheless, this has to be a pretty damn hot priority area to go for, doesn't it?

Scrap Rates

Finally, into our non-ferrous foundry, where the sand used is 'green' sand, not resin-bonded 'forane' sand. This next item is likely to be a bit of an anti-climax after the £295,392 a year saving potential next door, but it's important, just the same.

Green sand is used 'wet' for moulding. Water is added in small doses to make the moulding sand cling together. If the amount of water content is wrong, the sand will not cling together properly, and the result will be a scrap casting. There are lots of other reasons for scrap castings, of course, but it is commonly accepted that in green sand operations, 50% of the scrap rate is due to the water content of the moulding sand being wrong.

I spell this out because I didn't know this, and our management consultant found that a large proportion of our foundry personnel didn't know it either.

Can you imagine how I felt, therefore, when I also learned that the water content of our green sand was being measured by a rather traditional and crude method—the sand mixer was grabbing a handful of sand from time to time, squeezing, nodding sagely and muttering "that'll do!"

An accurate water dosing, measuring and control system could be fitted to our sand mixing equipment for around £6,500. This will theoretically reduce our casting scrap rate from its present 8% to a much happier 4%. On the amount of castings we produce a year, you can easily calculate what this 4% represents in money terms. Added to this, of course, will be a reduction in the need to do some of the jobs again, which lets our customers down on delivery.

That's just five examples then. There are probably fifty five more that we haven't found yet. And it occurs to me that, with such a lot of money at stake, we should get some kind of suggestion scheme going so that all our employees could help us improve things, and benefit themselves in some tangible proportion to the amount we save. I know our last suggestion scheme flopped, but maybe if we told everyone the kind of things we were looking for, and gave them these kind of examples, it would stand a much better chance of being a success.

Furthermore, these five examples also go to show the kind of ammunition a really good salesman has to use when he's trying to sell machine tools, or cooling towers, or expensive valves, or sand reclaimation plant, or water dosing equipment. Our products must show similar kinds of customer benefits in their own fields, but do our salesmen have and use this kind of ammunition? I doubt it—**YET!** See my treatment area titled "Converting more Quotations into Orders".

10–PRODUCTION EFFICIENCY
Your personal estimate of the percentage improvement possible.

Prices	Variable Costs
	(10%)
Sales	Fixed Costs

The figure in brackets is our management consultant's estimate of the probable percentage improvement in a business where this specific treatment area is a major problem.

Use this space for notes, calculations and to draft redundancy notices.

Money saved is better than money earned.

11–TOILET TIME

The following item appeared in the *Daily Telegraph* not long ago.

WALK-OUT OVER TOILET ORDER

About 150 soap factory workers struck yesterday, claiming that their management had ruled that they must ask permission to go to the toilet. The strikers also said their tea and cigarette breaks had been withdrawn.

The soap firm declined to comment.

Now I don't expect any of our enlightened managers to make such a silly mistake, but this news item does serve to highlight a particular problem which I am advised is costing this group an arm and a leg. And it is an incredibly complex problem, fraught with emotional difficulties and self-consciousness when management begins to look for improvements.

Toilet Time probably costs industry and commerce between 10% and 20% of its productivity. And most companies do nothing to combat this. The few that do wind up with a strike on their hands if they attack the problem with hobnailed boots.

There cannot be many authorities on the subject of Toilet Time. Our management consultant is one, and has passed to me a set of rules for reducing Toilet Time to a minimum and so increasing productivity. These rules apply to the factories, the offices **AND** the executive suites.

Rule One

If you want to make any progress at all, **don't get** nasty with the workers.

Don't remove the toilet paper, they'll bring their own and take longer on principle, or use the Sun after reading it.

Don't remove the seats, this will result in strained stomachs and increase time off work because of injury or illness.

Don't remove the light bulbs, this will create mess and the

toilet attendants will have to replace the light bulbs anyway to be able to see to clear up the mess.

Rule Two

Instead, minimise on the number of toilets you provide. One for every 15 staff is the rule for offices and factories employing female workers. For predominately male workers, increase the number of stand-up urinals and reduce the number of sit-upon cubicles, by agreement with your local factory inspector.

The fewer sit-ons you have, the less time you will lose.

Rule Three

Male workers are long-sitters.

Female workers are short-sitters but spend more time in total because they do their faces and adjust their stockings. So in male toilets, use light bulbs which make it difficult to read yet easy to operate. In female toilets provide plenty of light, but only small mirrors—**NOT** full length mirrors.

(The male toilet cubicle with the window will always be the most used. So brick up the window next time you re-decorate. Frosted glass doors also help cut down long sitting time, as does increasing the gap between door and floor from 4 inches to 8 inches.)

Rule Four

Office girls usually go to the toilet in pairs.

Reason is not for protection, but to gossip. So if you can, make it a rule that only **ONE** girl should be away from the job at any one time. This will cut out the gossip time and so reduce the overall toilet time.

Rule Five

In a predominantly female worker environment, get rid of the gloom-mongers. These are the old biddies who say to other female workers—"Doris, you do look tired today". Because Doris will go straight to the toilet to re-do her face and that's another ten minutes productively gone west.

Rule Six

Position toilets as close to the job as you can.

A survey was made about ten years ago of a construction site, by a supplier of portable toilets.

The construction site was a multi-storey office block, and

the portable toilet supplier was suggesting that to provide toilet facilities on each floor of the building while it was under construction would radically improve productivity. The construction firm was sceptical, and so the survey was conducted to measure how much time was wasted on trips to and from the toilets, which were positioned in a remote corner of the site.

Half a dozen "spotters" were discreetly positioned around the site for a week, some hidden, some with other jobs to do. At the end of the week it was established that Toilet Time accounted for 8 hours per week per man.

It was also established that it took **4 times as long** for a man to get back to his work station, as it took him to get **to** the toilet in the first place. (Okay, the sense of urgency had disappeared!)

The construction firm provided portable toilets on each floor of the building the very next working day.

Rule Seven

Don't scrimp on the quality of the toilet paper.

More than 50% of the over 40 population of the UK suffers from haemorrhoids. Shiny, single tissue makes male workers sit longer, thus aggravating both their personal problem and the productivity problem. Advocate double soft toilet tissue, but supply it in commercial size rolls which can be locked in special dispensers and thus do not get removed for use at home.

Rule Eight

The washroom towels **ARE** critically important. Not to management but to the workers. In a factory environment, towels become soiled and soaking wet very quickly. Continuous roll linen towels run out very fast. Complaints come fast, and these are the kinds of problems which cause unrest.

If you have these kinds of problems, get rid of the towels completely. Install hot air electric blower hand dryers. For around £120 each, they are a sound investment.

So those are the rules. I look to each of you to do what you can to minimise Toilet Time and so increase productive time—but **WITHOUT** causing the group any grief with its employees or the unions.

Finally, to point out that it isn't only the toilets that sap our strength; here's another new item from a recent *Daily Telegraph*:

"Workshy Britain came under the microscope yesterday as many other industries grimly realised that they are as slack as British Shipbuilders, where a survey has shown the average employee works for less than five hours out of each eight-hour shift.

British Shipbuilders itself announced an immediate campaign, with the backing of unions, to get a 10 per cent increase in productivity by cutting lost time from 185 to 30 minutes per day per man as a first target.

A check by a battery group with similar factories in Britain and Denmark found productivity was much poorer in Britain—mainly because tea breaks lasted longer, the start-up in the morning and after lunch was slower and the slow-down before the end of the shift came much earlier.

One survey of Ford factories in Britain and Belgium highlighted another cause of poor productivity in the United Kingdom.

In Belgium, maintenance engineers constantly walked the production line looking for possible breakdowns and putting things right immediately. In Britain, they stay in their room until a breakdown occurred and brought the line to a stand-still.

In many countries a working shift goes on until the last moment. In most British factories the production line slows down 15 minutes before the shift is due to end and workers queue up at the gate waiting to clock-off the moment the whistle goes.

It is just as bad in offices. The manager of a City insurance company department made an unofficial spot check yesterday and found many typists worked for little more than four hours.

The rest of the time was taken up with private telephone calls, lengthy visits to the lavatory, extend breaks, chatting to each other, late arrivals and early departures."

We appear to be just as bad as most in all these areas. See what improvements you can make. See what ideas you can come up with that you can share with the rest of us. We may need a special meeting on this subject. Should we hold it in the executive loo?

C.L. OAKROOM.
CHIEF TIMEWASTER

11–TOILET TIME

Your personal estimate of the percentage improvement possible.

Prices	Variable Costs
	(3%)
Sales	Fixed Costs
	(2%)

The figures in brackets are our management consultant's estimate of the probable percentage improvement in a business where this specific treatment area is a major problem.

Use this space for notes and calculations ONLY.

12–OFFICE FURNITURE

Most of our offices have been in existence for quite a few years. During this time, they have accumulated an impressive array of assorted items of furniture, filing aids, shelves, chairs, pots, coat stands, office machinery, desk paraphemalia, etc.—not all of it ever having appeared on the group's capital equipment inventories.

Frankly, the accumulation of such wealth—and what this does to office efficiency—had never occurred to me until our management consultant raised the question. But once the point has been made, it tends to hit you between the eyes.

We've never had a hierarchy system which dictates which executives have which grade of desk, chair and carpet—thank God. Similarly, there has never been any system which causes demarkation in our lower ranks. So human nature rules and, office staff all being avid collectors, each employee tends to acquire and then jealously guard any item of spare furniture or equipment that floats past during one of our many office re-organisations.

When anyone leaves, it's like a family reunion for a wake. After the body has been suitably despatched, the rest of the family fights over the estate—in our case all the furniture and fittings used by the departing member, except for the bare essentials. Thus, the acquisition of more "worldly goods" continues steadily, come what may.

No one worries about whether the furniture and equipment officially provided and unofficially acquired is suitable for doing the job most effectively. In fact, a few short months after any professional study of the needs and ergonomics of any particular department, resulting in the installation of the most efficient furniture and equipment, the staff of that department will be taking it all for granted once again and re-organising everything to suit their own personal tastes and habits—good or bad.

Surprise 'Em

Here is one way of solving the problem. It occupied a whole weekend for our management consultant and three of his staff, plus a 30 cwt. van.

Commencing 9.00 a.m. Saturday morning, every office in his 9000 square feet headquarters building was stripped to its bare essentials of office equipment and furniture. Strict attention was paid, of course, to the jobs which had to be done in each office. In certain cases, furniture in one office was exchanged for furniture in another office, to increase efficiency.

The exercise brought to light a number of efficiency reducing factors:-

1. Half the drawers in office desks are used for personal belongings rather than company stationery.
2. Ditto for cupboards.
3. Ditto for bookshelves.
4. Plant life often takes up 25% of the total working area of desks or tables.
5. Nothing—but nothing—is ever thrown away.
6. All those toilet rolls which had been assumed 'AWOL' were actually safe and sound in office cupboards or desk drawers, labelled "for emergency use only" or "in case of shortage or strike".

The furniture and equipment removed during the weekend, having been designated "un-necessary", filled a 50' warehouse.

The waste paper thrown away by the office staff—under instructions from above—during the ensuing two weeks filled a seven cubic yard skip.

The reaction of the office staff when they arrive for work on Monday morning following the secret removal operation was one of surprise rather than horror. They accepted the situation and, in a couple of hours, realised how much more elbow room they all had, and how this made the job easier to do.

Only two items of furniture had to be returned to offices from the warehouse. After four weeks, just to be sure, the rest was sold. The management also backed up the whole operation by replacing 6 tray plastic stationery units with 15 drawer

'Bisley' metal stationery cabinets, which took up the same amount of space but held three times as much stationery; providing copper and brass planters to replace margarine tubs; replacing assorted wall calendars with framed pictures and generally upgrading the working environment—at no cost, because the price obtained for the unnecessary furniture and equipment more than covers the upgrading costs.

The staff were pleased, and productivity improved significantly.

Your Way

Whether you adopt the same method as our management consultant, or get your entire staff working with you on the project, please take some action—because everyone of us has a dose of the "accumulated furniture" disease. (You've probably already noticed the results of my own office re-organisation exercise. Now you know why I did it.)

But take note. Do this one yourself. DO NOT DELEGATE IT. You're the boss, and only the boss can carry this one through without politics getting in the way.

12—OFFICE FURNITURE

Your personal estimate of the percentage improvement possible.

Prices	Variable Costs
Sales	Fixed Costs (1%)

This is a true 1% area. Rarely will any business gain more. But you can still try.

Use this space for notes, calculations and plans for the office layout.

13–TYPISTS AND SECRETARIES

We're short of typists and secretaries—desperately short.

Good ones, that is. Agreed?

Less and less good, reliable, conscientious girls are coming into business as typists and secretaries. Again, our over-education system and the ease by which 'O' level people can gain University places is leaving us with a large hole in the middle, between the 'thick' and the 'brilliant', just as it has done for technicians and craftsmen.

Note the words of Harry P. Cemach, from his book "A Farewell to Typists", on this subject:-

"If you have a typist, or the services of one, you probably often wonder whether you employ her—or she employs you.

When she's there, that is, and not on holiday, sick, feeling under the weather, late, gone off early, looking after a sick child/parent/husband/car.

(If only you could read that dictation on her pad which she left untyped).

There's hope, though. She'll be back eventually. Unless she's given notice that she won't be coming back.

Then the search starts again. Advertisements produce girls who can neither type nor spell. Agencies produce girls who can barely type and spell.

They interview you. (Come on, admit it!)

And maybe one stays for a while.

You show her what to do. Tell her where things are and dictate some letters.

When she brings them back, typed, you try to recall what you said in the first place, because any similarity between what she typed and what you dictated is purely coincidental".

The short answer to this has to be—"Let's make sure we don't lose the good typists and secretaries we already have". Because it is like Harry Cemach says.

How do we make sure we don't lose good girls?

Our management consultant says that, apart from the salary we have to pay to cut out the competition, it is simply a question of job satisfaction and interest, and equipment.

On job satisfaction and interest, I don't need to tell you what to do, and what to make sure your own people do. If your girls don't feel they are doing something important, some of them will get bored and quit.

On equipment, few good girls will be interested in another job if that job offers typewriter, desk, filing system, etc, inferior to those they are used to. So the best golfball electric typewriter, lateral filing, fully equipped desk, orthopaedic chair, real plants, not plastic, will keep a good girl long term for not much additional cost.

Check with my previous treatment area on "Office Furniture" though.

Back to Harry P. Cemach for another solution:-

"Some people believe there is a simple answer to the shortage of typists and secretaries. Let's have dictating machines, they say. No longer will typists waste time taking dictation. These machines save 50% of a typist's time.

This doesn't happen, however.

Give an executive a dictating machine and what does he do? Why, of course, he dictates more and more and more .... So whereas he needed one *secretary when he dictated to her, he now needs* two *typists to keep pace with his ever-increasing output of verbiage".*

Our management consultant only agrees with this in part. He claims that during the first euphoric few weeks of using a dictating machine, the average executive follows Cemach. After that, less than 20% learn to master the art of dictating and have typists and secretaries who grow to appreciate them. The other 80% plus gradually lose interest in the dictating machine and in six months are back to dicatating for shorthand.

He claims that half the dictating machines installed in businesses are hardly ever used. And that's a lot of capital tied up unnecessarily. The problem is further aggravated by the typists and secretaries themselves. If they have a shorthand capability, they want to keep it up. Six months without using shorthand and the average secretary will be hard pushed to tackle normal dictation.

Perhaps there is a need to match the right procedure to the right girl, or even mix dictating machines with shorthand.

Both our management consultant and Harry P. Cemach agree on one thing, however. The shortage of typists and secretaries is self-inflicted and could be ended tomorrow—not by finding more good girls but by installing better equipment and by cutting our superfluous typing.

If a secretary has to type regular long reports or sales quotations or similar, better than the golf-ball electric typewriter may be the daisy-wheel, floppy disc word-processor. For around £10,000 a machine can be purchased (or hired) which will type with unerring accuracy at 550 words per minute, match a list of names and addresses to a standard letter automatically and much more.

Such a machine will cope with the work load of three ordinary typewriters. One good girl instead of three. The quality of the output of letters will also be significantly improved. Used for sales quotations, the possibilities are enormous.

On superfluous typing, both our management consultant (who has examined the kind of letters we write) and Cemach claim our letters average 500 words and could be reduced to 200 words.

Why are they so long? Not enough thought about what we want to say, and why, before we dictate. Excessive use of "Victoriana" ("...thank you for your esteemed enquiry...") Rule—Write English as she is spoke. And keep it simple. Short sentences, short paragraphs. Plenty of punctuation. (There are 13 items of punctuation. How many do you know and how many do you use?)

We write a lot of letters explaining to people why we cannot do what they ask us to do (like sending a spare part) instead of just doing it. After all, if some one asks for a part, they don't want a letter, they want the part.

We could reply to a lot of letters on less important matters by handwriting the reply on the letter itself and returning it to the sender, plus a little sticker which says, "We reckon you will prefer this informal but instant reply" or "Please forgive the informality of this reply".

We could Telex more than we do, instead of writing 500 word letters.

We could increase our use of standard letters and complment slips.

We could use standard "Ping-Pong" no-carbon-required memo sets for our internal communications.

All this could reduce our requirement for typing and secretarial capacity by prodigious amounts. Estimate by how much for your own department and division.

Other Problems with Typists and Secretaries

There are two notorious vampires in our everyday world. One is Television—the only thing ever devised by man which creates and proliferates idleness. The other is the Photocopier.

Apart from the fact that there is no such thing as a **Reliable** Photocopier, the Photocopier is a device for multiplying pieces of paper, and it accomplishes this function magnificently, with the enthusiastic help and encouragement of just about everyone in UWC.

Every time we estimate the usage for a Photocopier in any department, the **ACTUAL** usage is at least double. Why is this? Why do we tolerate it? How did we manage to run our business **BEFORE** Photocopiers? Why do we use 70% less carbon paper now, compared with ten years ago?

If we threw all our Photocopiers out tomorrow, would our business grind to a halt? Of course it wouldn't.

So how do we reduce the use of Photocopiers, especially the use by our typists and secretaries, who used to use carbon paper?

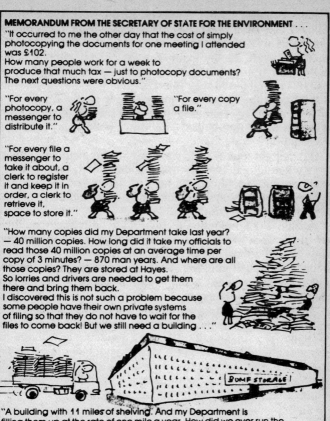

MEMORANDUM FROM THE SECRETARY OF STATE FOR THE ENVIRONMENT . . .

"It occurred to me the other day that the cost of simply photocopying the documents for one meeting I attended was £102.
How many people work for a week to produce that much tax — just to photocopy documents? The next questions were obvious."

"For every photocopy, a messenger to distribute it."

"For every copy a file."

"For every file a messenger to take it about, a clerk to register it and keep it in order, a clerk to retrieve it, space to store it."

"How many copies did my Department take last year? — 40 million copies. How long did it take my officials to read those 40 million copies at an average time per copy of 3 minutes? — 870 man years. And where are all those copies? They are stored at Hayes.
So lorries and drivers are needed to get them there and bring them back.
I discovered this is not such a problem because some people have their own private systems of filing so that they do not have to wait for the files to come back! But we still need a building . . ."

"A building with 11 miles of shelving. And my Department is filling them up at the rate of one mile a year. How did we ever run the greatest empire the world ever saw without photocopiers? Rather better I suspect than we run our country today."

MICHAEL HESELTINE

First published in NOW! MARCH 28, 1980, and re-printed here

by kind permission of the publishers.

Next problem is the Holiday Rota. Like every other business, we have work-load problems during the holiday period due to key staff being on holiday at the same time as other key staff in the same department. It should never happen, but it does. And usually we don't even know about it until it is too late—and they've gone.

We have rules about how many people in any department can go on holiday at the same time, don't we? And we operate on a 'first come, first served' basis, don't we? So why is there a problem?

Out of sight, out of mind, says our management consultant. What we need is a departmental Holiday Chart, on a wall for all to see, and next to it, the holiday rules. Then, no-one will be able to abuse the system, innocently or deliberately.

Damnably simple, isn't it?

Finally, a 1% reduction of production efficiency could be put at the door of some of our senior typists and secretaries, who appear to delight in walking through our production shops in very tight sweaters. Every time this happens, concentration reduces and scrap rate increases. You know what shop-floor workers are.

Try to stop your girls taking short cuts through the production shops. Or delegate message carrying to less attractive girls.

13—TYPISTS, SECRETARIES, PHOTOCOPIERS
Your personal estimate of the percentage improvement possible.

Prices	Variable Costs
Sales	Fixed Costs (3%)

The figure in brackets is our management consultant's estimate of the probable percentage improvement in a business where this specific treatment area is a major problem.

Use this space for notes and calculations. Please be brief!

TREATMENT AREAS
FOR
RAISING
PRICES
and cutting discounts

14—ARBITRARY PRICE INCREASES

There is much less to say about treatment areas for raising prices and cutting discounts. The actual problems are simpler, and action is easier to take.

One thing we must all get clear. There is nothing to prevent us from increasing our prices, just for the hell of it, totally unconnected with the cost side of our business. (Barring Government intervention as during the years 1974—78.) Price has no direct relationship to cost. Price is set according to what the customers can be persuaded to pay. Price is **not** according to what our competitors are doing, providing we can justify to our customers why they should pay more.

Of course, we need to offer good value for money and good service. We would also have extreme difficulties if we put prices up too high too quickly, as any business would.

In implementing any reasonable but still arbitrary price increase, there are really only two hurdles to clear:-

1. Informing the customers in a way which they will readily accept.
2. Overcoming 'Price Fright' in our own people. (This I will deal with in the next treatment area.)

Informing customers about price increases is a selling skill all of its own. There has to be a sound, logical reason for increasing prices, and this reason must be conveyed to the customers in a way which they will accept. This normally involves giving other information to back up the decision to increase prices, information designed to keep the customers happy to stay with us.

Our management consultant has provided me with a couple of examples of the art of writing good price increase letters—see pages 91 and 92. They speak for themselves, and the company concerned goes from strength to strength.

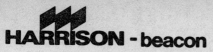

HARRISON - beacon

Harrison Beacon Ltd. P.O. Box 233 Bradford Street Birmingham B12 0PE England
Telephone 021-772 3421 Telex 338823 (DIYKIN G)
Telegrams REMARKABLE

Please note our new telephone number is: 021 773 1111

Our ref: DKWH:ef   2nd January, 1979.

Dear Sirs:

We would advise that with effect from midnight on the 7th January, 1979,
our prices will rise by an average of 3.16% across our full product range.
Pursuant to our Terms of Trading, all goods despatched subsequent to that
time, will be at the new prices.

Whilst the percentage quoted is across our full product range, we are pleased
to advise that no Hardware items have been increased. We have taken the
decision not to increase Hardware prices in the light of the poor availability
of product over the last six months. We feel that we must accept this cost
and trust that the action will be recognised.

The effect of increasing staff, overtime and extra shift work is now beginning
to pay off and you can at last look forward to an improving availability.

We thank you for your support in 1978 and look forward to a successful 1979.

Yours sincerely,

D.K.W. Hanratty - DIRECTOR

A member of the McKechnie group of companies. Reg. Office: PO Box 8 Longhswood Road Aldridge Walsall West Midlands WS9 8DS Reg No. 650632 England

HARRISON - beacon

Harrison Beacon Ltd. P.O. Box 233 Bradford Street Birmingham B12 0PE England
Telephone 021-773 1111 Telex 338823 (DIYKIN.G)
Telegrams REMARKABLE

Our ref: DKWH:ef   28th March, 1979.

Dear Sirs:

We would advise that with effect from midnight on the 1st April, 1979, our
price will rise on Hardware Products by an average of 12%. Pursuant to our
Terms of Trading, all goods despatched subsequent to that time, will be at
the new prices.

We advised in our letter to you in January that Hardware would not be increased
in price until our service levels had improved.   At that time our service
across all Hardware Products was 66% and on the more popular lines as low
as 40%.   We are pleased to report that our service levels across all Hardware
Products is now 83% and on the more popular lines 77%.   We are still improving
on this percentage.

The 783/784 Carpet Gripper, whilst in the price list, is discontinued, and no
more orders can be accepted for this product.

We thank you for your patience.

Yours sincerely,

D.K.W. Hanratty - DIRECTOR

N.B.   CURTAIN RAIL PRODUCTS ARE <u>NOT</u> INCREASED IN PRICE.

A member of the McKechnie group of companies. Reg. Office: PO Box 8 Leighswood Road Aldridge Walsall West Midlands WS9 8DS. Reg. No. 850632 England

H. 70

But note please the interesting average 3.16% increases. Such a figure must have been very carefully calculated indeed. The credibility of the increase is assured. Much better than a 5% round figure, even though the increase of each **item** in the product range will be a round figure.

Government Threats to our GM

We may never see a situation like 1974—78 again, when the Government puts the handcuffs on companies and stops them increasing prices without express permission—permission gained only after several months of hard work, many weary meetings and much form filling.

But just in case it happens again, here is a standing order:-

Keep very close watch on the Consumer Prices Index and the Retail Prices Index. And on any other official price index which matters to our business. In time of Government price control, claim for everything that keeps us level with the CPI and RPI increases—monthly, quarterly, half yearly and annually— and claim **FAST**.

Put the group in a position where it gets approval for the maximum allowable price increase, faster than its competitors. Once we are in this position, we don't necessarily have to implement the approved price increase, but it is a hell of a nice feeling to know that when the time comes to actually put up the prices—we don't have to wait another six months while we go through the official channels.

This way, we get the best of both worlds **and** protect our margins.

I have linked this treatment area with the next one. It is pointless implementing an arbitrary price increase unless you can also overcome 'Price Fright'. Thus, any improvement of Profit will come **then**, not here, and that is where you will find the next personal estimate box.

15–OVERCOMING "PRICE FRIGHT"

We are afraid of our prices!

To successfully implement an arbitrary price increase—or any kind of price increase for that matter—we have to cure this ailment.

If our products are really good, as we all know they are, we should be **PROUD** of our prices. We should be able to sell them with confidence against any competition. We should be able to justify to any customer why he should pay more and what he gets for the additional money our products cost.

If we cannot, our sales training and product training, for salesforce and sales office personnel alike, must be at fault.

Few customers today buy only on price. They buy on quality, on reliability, on performance, on lower running costs, lower handling costs, lower maintenance costs, longer life, on service, on the availability of spares, on reputation, on all round best value for money.

Make sure all your sales personnel realise this—and know how to show our customers they get more for their money if they buy from eg UWC. More than this—make sure they **BELIEVE** it, for if they don't, if they feel you're kidding, they'll never generate the confidence and enthusiasm to put it over successfully to the customers.

This has to be your top priority sales training objective, for many other things stem from this one key issue.

Here is a little quotation which our management consultant has passed to me, and which all our sales personnel should have:-

"When you buy on price you can never be sure. It's unwise to pay too much, but it's worse to pay too little. When you pay too much you lose a little money, that's all. But when you pay too little, you sometimes lose everything.

Because the little you bought is incapable of doing the thing it was bought to do.

The common law of business balance prohibits paying a little and getting a lot.
It can't be done.
If you deal with the lowest bidder, it is well to add something for the risk you run, and if you do that you will have enough to buy **Quality.**"

14/15—OVERCOMING 'PRICE FRIGHT'

Your personal estimate of the percentage improvement possible.

Prices (5%)	Variable Costs
Sales (10%)	Fixed Costs

The figures in brackets are our management consultant's estimate of the probable percentage improvement in a business where this specific treatment area is a major problem.

Use this space for notes and calculations.

16–PRICING FOR MAXIMUM PROFIT

Our pricing policies are suspect. They're not bad, but it would appear that we have never grasped the key fundamental issue and decided precisely what we want to go for.

There are three things we can go for:-

Maximum volume of products sold, by unit of product.

Maximum volume of sales, by value.

Maximum profit contribution.

Snag is, it is not possible to achieve **all three** of them.

It would be easy for me to say to you here and now—go for maximum profit and revise your pricing policies accordingly. But this might be wrong for some of our divisions, although right for others.

We have a few conflicts of interests lying around UWC.

In some of our divisions, production wants prices kept down so that unit volume can be increased and machines kept running, avoiding trouble with the unions because of insufficient overtime, shift fluctuations and lay-offs. A valid point.

In most of our divisions, the salesforce wants prices kept down (but not as far down as production) so that sales turnover can be maximised, because our sales targets and commission schemes are set mostly according to sales turnover by value.

Our directors invariably are interested mainly in profit, because we have outside shareholders to whom we have to give dividends and thus keep them happy. And because profit provides the resources with which UWC expands.

Quite often, therefore, the same price for our products will not satisfy all three of these interests.

So all I can say to you is—go for maximum profit wherever you can. And see if our sales targets and commission schemes can be changed from "sales turnover achieved" to "profit contribution achieved". (This will help you stop your salesforce) giving discounts away, as well).

If we price for maximum profit, we will automatically be reducing our sales turnover by value and our production volume by unit.

If we push for maximum volume, above a certain point, our profit will inevitably reduce. That's life.

No way am I going to tell you which to do or how to do it. Calculating your prices is a very complex business, involving a number of estimates and forecasts which only the people closest to the action are able to do with the required accuracy. So it's up to you. But here is one example (see page 99) given by our management consultant which demonstrates a few of the things that come out of these kinds of pricing calculations.

It should be noted that, contrary to this example, in most instances, the 'marginal unit cost' will vary inversely with the volume. But this is rarely a smooth variation. Thus, the steady 70 in the example is unlikely to be found in your own calculations.

1	2	3	4	5	6
Selling Price £	Volume Units	Turnover £K (1x2)	Marginal Unit Cost £	Total Cost £K (4x2)	Contribution £K (3–5)
100	40,000	4,000	70	2,800	1,200
110	35,000	3,800	70	2,450	1,400
122	32,500	3,965	70	2,275	1,690
130	31,000	4,030	70	2,170	1,860
150	26,000	3,900	70	1,820	2,080
180	15,000	2,700	70	1,050	1,650

16—PRICING FOR MAXIMUM PROFIT
Your personal estimate of the percentage improvement possible.

Prices	Variable Costs
(2%)	
Sales	Fixed Costs

The figure in brackets is our management consultant's estimate of the probable percentage improvement in a business where concern for maximum sales volume and fear of the competition has clouded the true situation. Thus, an increase in price would have negligible effect on sales volume.

Use this space for notes and calculations.

17–QUANTITY DISCOUNTS

Some of our sales personnel—and some of our executives—have lost sight of what a Quantity Discount is supposed to be. The word "Quantity" has somehow gotten lost. Only the word "Discount" remains, and is being used somewhat indiscriminately.

Discounts of any kind have to be paid for. They either get paid for out of savings made in our costs, or they get paid for out of our profit margin.

Quantity Discounts should be paid for out of savings made in our costs. If we make more of the product there will be a reduction in the unit cost. Customers know this and therefore expect to pay less if they buy more.

But many customers ask for discounts when they are not prepared to buy sufficient of the product to warrant a discount. And we are all too often guilty of letting them get away with it. Maybe because our competitors are also doing it, but that is no excuse. Worse than this, our salesmen don't work very hard to avoid giving such discounts. In fact, they sometimes **offer** a discount at an early stage of the sales interview. Our management consultant actually witnessed this. If I'd been there, I'd have fired the salesmen on the spot. But perhaps it would have been fairer to have fired his manager.

All our salesmen should have a table of true 'Quantity' discounts which apply to their products. Over and above this, the only discounts they should give are ones for which there is an equivalent **real** saving in costs. They should know where these savings in cost can be made, and learn how to use them to maximise sales, **and** to maximise profit.

For example, savings might be made if bulk transport is used instead of our normal transport, or if the customer has his own transport and can collect the goods from us. Savings might be made on special orders if materials can be purchased in bulk or improved production techniques used in the manufacture of the goods. In our distribution divisions this is much easier to see and to use to good effect.

Timing differences on deliveries can give savings. If our van is fully loaded rather than its normal half loaded, there is a genuine saving on our normal costings for the half loaded van. So if a customer is willing to wait another week or two for delivery, a small discount might be valid.

Airlines are good examples of this. Standard air fares are based on 60% occupancy. Charter fares are based on full occupancy. The cost of operating the aircraft is the same. The price per unit (the fare) is significantly different. Likewise, with hotel bedrooms and rates for individuals and for company conferences.

What can you do in your division to minimise the 'quantity' discounts we give away?

17—QUANTITY DISCOUNTS

Your personal estimate of the percentage improvement possible.

Prices	Variable Costs
(5%)	
Sales	Fixed Costs

The figure in brackets is our management consultant's estimate of the probable percentage improvement in a business where most new customers ask for a discount and normally are granted one indiscriminately, and where this problem could be resolved by the salesmen gently refusing by saying, "We've never given our long-standing big customers discounts over the normal trading terms—what do you think they would think of us if they found out we'd given **you** *a larger discount?"*

Use this space for notes and calculations

18–SETTLEMENT DISCOUNTS

This one we can lay at the door of our accounts departments.

A number of our divisions offer settlement discounts for payment of invoices within 30 days. At least one division gives a larger discount for payment within 7 days, and for cash.

But customers are alive to the fact that whether they pay within 30 days, or 7 days, or what, they can still deduct our settlement discount and get away with it.

This is costing us money. And on regular accounts it would not cost us much at all to rigidly enforce our terms on which a settlement discount can be rightfully deducted.

So let's do it—right across the group. A simple letter to all customers, along the lines of the sample below, is all the paving-of-the-way we need.

Better than this—isn't it time we reviewed why the hell we're giving settlement discounts away in the first place? Would we lose much business if we operated on a strictly net monthly account basis? I suspect not. Look into it carefully, ready for a policy meeting and decision next month.

TO:— Accounts Payable Controller.

Dear Sir/Madam,

Cash Discounts

Our standard Terms of Trade have included the following clause since 1974:-

'Terms of Payment'

Accounts are due for payment not later than 30 days from date of invoice, and a cash discount is allowed if payment is received by us before the due date.

We have not vigorously applied these terms, but from the 2nd April 1981 cash settlement discount will only be allowed on invoices paid by the 21st of the month following date of invoice. The amount of discount will be shown on each invoice.

Any discount claimed against cash received after that date will be disallowed, i.e.—Accounts paid other than by 21st will be strictly nett.

If you have any queries regarding the claiming of discount, please contact our Mr. A.F. Wood, Credit Controller.

Yours faithfully,
B.W. UNWIN.
FINANCIAL DIRECTOR.

18—SETTLEMENT DISCOUNTS

Your personal estimate of the percentage improvement possible.

Prices (1%)	Variable Costs
Sales	Fixed Costs

The figure in brackets is our management consultant's estimate of the probable percentage improvement possible in the average business—so limited because of the number of immovable objects and insurmountable obstacles found in the average accounts department.

Use this space for notes and calculations.

19–MINIMUM ORDER VALUE

Are our minimum order values too low?

When did we last increase them?

If we increased them now, would we lose any business?

The question of minimum order values links closely with my treatment area on "Analysing Customers for Profit Contribution". If indeed we have a multitude of customers giving us small orders at little profit margin, then perhaps an increase in the minimum order value will give us a corresponding increase in profit and any customers we lose in the process we could be well rid of.

To invoice **anything** in our product range costs us at least £5. Probably more. It has been suggested that a £50 minimum order value would be feasible for our industrial consumables products, and a £25 or £30 minimum order value for our retailing business, instead of our £20 and £10 respectively m.o.v's now.

Check my comments on "Packaging" as well, before you reach any final decision. You may be able to change the standard quantities or sizes per order and increase the value of each order secured, at the same time as increasing the m.o.v.

M.O.V. can reduce costs and increase sales. It's not strictly a price increase or discount treatment area but it fits better into this section, so here it is.

19—MINIMUM ORDER VALUE

Your personal estimate of the percentage improvement possible.

Prices	Variable Costs
	(5%)
Sales	Fixed Costs
(5%)	(5%)

The figures in brackets are our management consultant's estimate of the probable percentage improvement in a business where the majority of customers place small orders and the Minimum Order Value is either non-existent or hasn't been increased for ten years.

Use this space for notes and calculations

When all is said and done, there's more said than done.

TREATMENT AREAS FOR
INCREASING SALES

20–THE ADVERTISING BUDGET

Why do we need to advertise at all? We have salesmen, sales literature—why not leave it to them?

Questions like that have been asked for years by probably every company in the land. I've heard them asked many times in UWC. I've never been able to give anyone a completely convincing reply, but I've always had a feeling in my water that we **should** advertise, and advertise we certainly do.

Now I have some valid, more precise reasons. Happily, that feeling in my water was correct.

We advertise mainly to generate enquiries for our products which our salesmen can subsequently follow up and convert into orders. We do this because our salesmen haven't time to bang on enough doors. This much we always knew. We also knew that banging on doors was a lousy way to sell UWC products anyway, and uneconomical.

But consider these findings from a recent survey of some 1100 companies of all types and sizes:-

First, how do people in our customer companies gather the information they need to make their buying decisions? This is what the survey revealed:-

Information Source	Small Companies (1 to 400 employees)	Large Companies (401 to 1000 + employees)
Trade and Technical Press Advertising	28%	60%
Salesmens' visits	45%	19%
Exhibitions	8%	12%
Direct Mail shots	19%	9%

So there is a second reason we need to advertise.

Now, how many people in our customer companies

influence, or play a part in, the average decision to buy something? This is what the survey revealed:-

Company Size, by number of employees	Average number of decision influencers	Number of influencers visited by salesmen
Less than 200	3.43	1.72
200 to 400	4.85	1.75
401 to 1000	5.81	1.90
1001 and over	6.50	1.65

So if we are trading around the average, our salesmen are not even seeing *half* the decision influencers they should be seeing. Often, it's no fault of theirs; some customers won't tell them who else to see, or let them see them if they do find out.

How do we get at these unvisited decision influencers? Through advertising, backed up by trade exhibitions, direct mail shots and PR. So that's three reasons so far.

But that is only the tip of the iceberg when it comes to problems with our advertising budgets. Our management consultant asked me how we decided on the amount of money we spent on advertising. He gave me a list of six methods to pick from:-

1. *% of last year's turnover*
2. *% of next year's forecast sales*
3. *% of profit*
4. *Keeping up with the Competition*
5. *"Task" method*
6. *"Guvnor's whim"*

It doesn't really matter which method we have been using. What matters is that only 5, "Task" method, is the right method. All the rest are totally wrong. What do I mean by "Task method"? It means establishing what you want to achieve in finite terms, and then costing it out and arriving at a budget. If this budget is obviously too high, pruning can then be done on an objective basis. Without this objectivity, the likelihood is that the available money will be spread over all aspects of sales promotion, not just advertising, and

113

probably nothing meaningful will be achieved in any aspect.

Now a well-known quotation, by the first Lord Leverhulme, talking about his company, Lever Brothers.

"Half the money we spend on advertising is wasted.
The only problem is, we don't know which half!"

This is still true, more often than not, today. So how do we narrow down the odds in our favour?

First consider the purpose of an advertisement. There can be three—

Prestige for the Company

Generating Enquiries for the Product

Maintaining Belief in the Product

Most of the time, in our advertisements, we should be attempting to fulfil all three purposes. This is quite possible.

To make sure our advertisements are effective and the money they cost is not part of Lord Leverhulme's wasted half, we need to consider **all** the phases of what our advertisement has to do:-

1. *Exposure* (*picking the right media*)
2. *Perception* (*choosing a position which the reader will see*)
3. *Retention* (*getting the message across*)
4. *Decision* (*getting the reader to Act, in our favour*)

Looking at 2, 3 and 4 in a man to man way (us and the reader), what we have to achieve is this:-

A *Rapport* (*make him smile, frown or raise his eyebrows*)
B *Unfreeze* (*make him doubt his preconceived views*)
C *Move* (*make him curious and then interested about us*)
D *Refreeze* (*make him feel we are a better preconceived view*)

If we do not complete **ALL** these phases, the chances are we will be wasting the money we spend.

All this gave me a completely fresh outlook on our advertising, and made me confident that we can both save some money and get much better results in future. I hope you will feel the same.

Revised budgets for the rest of this year's advertising will be happily received at next month's meeting.

114

20—THE ADVERTISING BUDGET

Your personal estimate of the percentage improvement possible.

Prices	Variable Costs
Sales (10%)	**Fixed Costs** (3%)

The figures in brackets are our management consultant's estimate of the probable percentage improvement in a business where decisions on advertisements are made by a committee consisting of the Advertising Agency, the Chairman, his wife and her gardener. The gardener's opinion usually prevails. (If you use an Agency, brief them properly and then leave it to them—that's what you are paying for.)

Use this space for notes and calculations.

21–GETTING OUR SERVICE ENGINEERS TO SELL

This one hit me straight between the eyes—it's such common sense.

Our service engineers are in constant face-to-face communication with our customers; not just the decision makers, but the people who actually use our products.

Yet we never encourage them to **SELL** anything. We never teach them how to go about anything except repairing the product when it goes wrong. We fail even to teach them what to do when the product is almost worn out and due for replacement.

Service engineers are in an ideal position to **RECOMMEND** to customers a course of action which gives us business. And customers listen to a service engineer as a technician, an engineer, an expert, not as a salesman who is bound to be biased in favour of what he is selling.

Service engineers can feed back information to our salesmen on when to go in and sell again, and on what product to concentrate. Yet our service engineers rarely do this. More often, there is a kind of cold war existing between the service department and the sales department—a classic US and THEM situation.

Service engineers bear the brunt of customers' complaints. They invariably get called in when things have gone wrong. Yet do we teach them how to properly handle customer complaints? Do we hell!

From our service engineers could be grown our salesmen of tomorrow yet we do nothing to prepare our engineers for this logical promotion step, and so we lose all round.

What we **should** be doing is getting our service engineers involved in our sales training sessions; sending selected engineers on outside salesmanship and customer relations courses. Bringing them into sales meetings, especially meetings which discuss major customers.

We should be making our service engineers feel important—because they **ARE** important.

Let me have your detailed proposals for getting **YOUR** service engineers to sell, by the end of next month.

Service engineers...

> *...meet decision makers*
> *...meet users who are rarely seen by salemen*
> *...can recommend replacement of competitors equipment with ours*
> *...can sell spares, repairs, their time, maintenance contracts customer training.*

21—GETTING OUR SERVICE ENGINEERS TO SELL

Your personal estimate of the percentage improvement possible.

Prices	Variable Costs
Sales (5%)	Fixed Costs (2%)

The figures in brackets are our management consultant's estimate of the probable percentage improvement in a business where this specific treatment area is a major problem.

Use this space for notes and calculations.

22–PERFORMANCE APPRAISAL

All our employees, executives down to shop floor, will only give of their best if they can see they are getting somewhere, and if that "somewhere" is where they want to go. This is called Personal Development.

If we can get some cost saving mileage out of Recruiting the Right People, it seems logical that, having recuited better people (round pegs for our round holes) we should keep the thing going by making sure these people give of their best—long term.

The key element in Personal Development is what is called the Appraisal Interview. This is an annual, or better still once every six months, meeting between an employee and his manager, at which the immediate past performance of the employee is reviewed, objectives set and agreed for remedial action to resolve any problems, and timetable agreed for the next stage in the development plan for the employee.

Personal Development is critically important to every kind of employee, even our senior executives, but none so critical as our sales staff, because demotivation, demoralisation, a lack of a sense of real purpose, these things have a direct effect on our sales volume faster than anything else and, once the effect has taken hold, it's the devil's own job to boost things up again.

We don't appear to have any of these kinds of problems—yet. But we don't appear to have any kind of formal or informal Personal Development programmes either—nor do we appear to hold any Appraisal Interviews.

I don't want to risk the group degenerating in any way because we were negligent on a thing like this, so PD programmes for all—starting with the sales force and sales management—and Appraisal Interviews as soon as you can implement them with confidence that they will be run correctly.

How to make sure? Well, there is a film to help us on

Recruiting the Right People and there is another film to help us on Appraisal Interviewing. Again produced by Video Arts Ltd, Dumbarton House, 68 Oxford Street, London WIN 9LA, the film is titled "How Am I Doing?" and we will be seeing next month, along with "Man Hunt".

Meanwhile, here are some guideline notes on the principles of the Appraisal Interview:-

The Objectives of the Appraisal Interview:

to provide the person being appraised with feedback on how the company views him

to manage through agreed objectives (MBO)

to provide a basis for salary reviews

to provide career advice

to help career planning

to reduce 'aggro' and prejudice between manager and managed

to facilitate handover of staff or duties between managers

to avoid trouble, legal or otherwise.

Who should be Appraised?

Everyone should be. Any exceptions are bound to be known and cause problems.

Who Does the Appraising?

Next one up in the line management hierarchy, or two up if necessary, but no more than two, otherwise the appraiser will not be close enough in touch with what goes on, day to day.

Who Sees the Appraisal Results?

One up only from the appraiser, and the person being appraised, who should sign the appraisal as having seen and agreed the results. He should also be allowed to express his opinion, in writing, about any areas of development.

How Often?

A minimum of once a year—but once every six months is better, and more frequently than that if there is a specific problem to resolve.

How Performance Standards are Set

Before an Appraisal Interview can be successfully conducted finite standards of performance must be established for the person to be appraised. These standard must be objective, not subjective, must genuinely relate to the success or failure of the job, be easy for the appraiser to administer, and be seen to be fair.

Here is an example (see pages 122 and 123) of part of a set of Performance standards given me by our management consultant and which could well apply to our salesmen and be used by our sales managers. You will see that nowhere in the "Needs Improvement" columns can any salesman be labelled as really bad on any performance factor. This is critically important when setting performance standards, otherwise the whole exercise can quickly degenerate into a hatchet meeting—with disastrous results.

PRAISE is the all important word in leadership and management, even when you know the person being praised can do a lot better—and you tell him so.

SELLING SKILLS

1 PLANNING PREPARATION	ABOVE STANDARD	STANDARD	NEEDS IMPROVEMENT
a) Information	Has all the relevant information for every call	Has most of the relevant information for every call	Has some relevant information for most calls
b) Sales tools	Always carried all relevant equipment, stationery etc.	Invariably carried some relevant equipment, stationery etc.	Often carried some relevant equipment, stationery etc.
c) Action plan	Always prepared detailed action plan	Invariably prepares action plan	Often prepares an action plan
2 APPROACH			
a) Opening remarks	Always gains attention by using skilful opening phrases and "carrots"	Occasionally fails to gain attention because of failure to use "carrots"	Seldom uses "carrots" or skilful opening phrases
b) Sales aids	Always uses a sales aid where appropriate	Often uses a sales aid in approach	Seldom uses a sales aid in approach
3 PRESENTATION			
a) Product knowledge	Fully conversant with all products and applications	Well informed about all products and applications	Has some knowledge of most products and applications
b) Selling points	Knows and uses all selling points for all products	Knows most selling points for all products	Knows some selling points for most products
c) Buyer benefits	Always translates selling points into benefits	Occasionally fails to translate selling points into benefits	Sometimes translates selling points into benefits
d) Buying motives	Always makes presentation appeal to buyers motives	Occasionally fails to make presentation appeal to buyers motives	Often fails to make presentation appeal to buyers motives
e) Sales aids	Always uses them to maximum advantage	Always uses them, often to maximum advantage	Sometimes uses sales aids, to advantage
f) Handling objections	Always handles objections successfully, leaving the buyer satisfied	Handles most objections successfully leaving the buyer satisfied	Handles some objections successfully, does not always leave the buyer satisfied
g) Selling sequence	Always uses correct sequence	Often uses correct sequence	Seldom uses correct sequence
h) Rental	Always endeavours to sell Rental	Often endeavours to sell Rental	Seldom endeavours to sell Rental
4 CLOSING THE SALE			
a) Buying signals	Always recognises and acts upon buying signals	Occasionally fails to recognise and act upon buying signals	Often fails to recognise and act upon buying signals
	Always uses the most appropriate style of close	Occasionally fails to use the appropriate style of close	Often fails to use the appropriate style of close
c) Departure drill	Always thanks, reassures or questions buyer as appropriate	Occasionally fails to thank, reassure or question the buyer as appropriate	Often fails to thank, reassure or question the buyer as appropriate

Figure 10. A guide to the salesman's performance appraisal record form shown in figure 11.

	ABOVE STANDARD	STANDARD	NEEDS IMPROVEMENT
5 CALL ANALYSIS			
a) Records/reports and Correspondence	Always completed accurately, promptly and up to date	Occasionally fails to complete accurately, promptly and up to date	Always completed but not always accurate, prompt and up to date
b) Information	Always records information for future use	Occasionally fails to record information for future use	Sometimes records information for future use
c) Self analysis	Invariably analyses personal performance	Often analyses personal performance	Seldom analyses personal performance
6 TERRITORY MANAGEMENT			
a) Use of selling time	Plans very carefully and wastes no time	Plans carefully, and wastes little time	Does not plan, and wastes time on unnecessary journeys
b) Competitors Activities	Actively seeks relevant information and keeps everybody informed	Generally good at reporting information	Seldom reports competitor activity
c) Territory Development	Constantly active and opening new a/cs in addition to developing existing a/cs	Developing existing a/cs and Occasionally opening new a/cs	Inclined to concentrate on existing business seldom trying to gain new customers
7 PERSONAL			
a) Appearance	Always exceptionally well turned out, and a credit to his company	Always well turned out and a credit to his company	Not always well turned out and a credit to the company
b) Attitude	Always expresses a positive attitude towards the company its products, policies, and its customers	Occasionally fails to express a positive attitude towards the company its products, policies, and its customers	Often expresses a negative attitude towards the company its products, policies and its customers
8 OTHER RELEVANT POINTS			

(continuation of figure 10)

A Warning

There is no doubt in the minds of personnel experts that the Appraisal Interview is one of the most effective tools with which a business can keep its employees interested, satisfied, motivated and committed.

However, there is equally no doubt that far too few Appraisal Interviews achieve these desirable results. Many result in so much bafflement, frustration and alienation that it would have been much better if they hadn't taken place at all.

The trouble is that most Appraisal Interviews are not conducted by trained personnel experts, they are conducted by busy line managers who are trained in different disciplines and who are beset by many other urgent problems. Worst of all, these managers do not think of the Appraisal Interview as a special event, nor that doing it successfully involves a new skill that has to be acquired. So when the interview is over, they feel it went pretty well and don't ever realise that the interviewee has gone off unhappy and dissatisfied, frustrated and wondering what it was all supposed to be in aid of.

To get it right, think of it as a doctor giving an over-weight patient his annual check-up. The doctor has to read up the case-history, he has to convince the patient of the need to lose weight, he has to get his agreement to an acceptable way of doing it, and he has to be straight with him about past errors and future dangers.

Medicine or management, it's just the same.

Only a mediocre person is always at his best.

Somerset Maugham

22—PERFORMANCE APPRAISAL

Your personal estimate of the percentage improvement possible.

Prices	Variable Costs
	(5%)
Sales	**Fixed Costs**
(5%)	(5%)

The figures in brackets are our management consultant's estimate of the probable percentage improvement in a business where this specific treatment area is a major problem.

Use this space for notes and calculations.

23–TRAINING IN MONEY MATTERS

Our modern business world is competitive, sophisticated and specialised. Only those of our staff who have been adequately trained will succeed.

Our management consultant has been looking into our training programmes, those he can find, that is, because sad to say, he reports that they are pretty near non-existent in most of our divisions.

We are not, he says, developing the potential of the people we employ. We have no clear idea where we want our key people to be in five years time, and therefore what we need to do to get them there. Because of this, we are losing more people than we should, and this is costing us a great deal of money. Furthermore, our replacements are quite often as unsuccessful as our attempts to keep the people who left us.

We cannot start soon enough to improve on this. Here are a few action examples to start you thinking.

Understanding Money

Very few of our salesmen really understand how money works in business—how a company funds its operations—how it makes its decisions on whether or not to buy capital items: how it calculates the financial and economical (and political) effects of increasing or decreasing its production capacity or its workforce; what the options are when seeking sources of finance; how the cash flow relates to those kinds of decisions—and so on.

Our salesforce on capital equipment, the machine tool and handling systems divisions, for example, must be on this ball if they are to successfully sell our products.

And they are **NOT**.

They know precious little about the money side of business, and this also applies to their managers.

Some examples of how this kind of knowledge can be applied by our capital equipment salesmen can be found in the

Cost Reduction section under "Production Efficiency".

Tools for Competitive Selling

Our salesmen on machine tools are not only selling against stiff competition, they are also selling a high priced, quality product against competitors who can offer much lower prices than we can.

We know this. We also know that some customers buy on price, rather than best quality or best value for money. Yet do we do anything to help our salesmen overcome these kinds of obstacles? Do we provide them with any tools to help convince this kind of customer he should buy from us at a much higher price?

No. We expect our salesmen to fend for themselves. And because of this, we lose orders we could have otherwise won.

Here is an example of a check list which we could give our machine tool salesmen for when they are trying to change the attitudes of a customer who usually buys the lowest priced product. The check list not only acts as a selling tool—it also helps **TRAIN** the salesman into thinking commercially, rather than technically, about the customer's objectives.

The selling technique for using this kind of check list is called "Criteria for Ordering", and it is a real dilly for making a reluctant customer consider in detail all the reasons why he should pay for a better product, rather than buy the cheapest.

Salesman to Customer:-

When you are choosing a Machine Tool supplier, what are the most important factors you consider before reaching a decision? What is your "Criteria for ordering"? (pauses, then shows customer his check list).

How many factors on our list fit your supplier criteria?

1. *The supplier has to be able to supply a machine which will do the job you want done.*
2. *And at the right time, to dovetail into your production programme.*
3. *And at the right price, to fit your budget.*
   Or alternatively, the supplier can provide hire purchase facilities so that you can install the machine NOW, and have it earning money for you while you are paying for it.

128

4. *The supplier should be able to offer realistic trade-in prices for any machine tools you are replacing.*
5. *The supplier should be able to supply not just a basic machine, but a whole range of accessories and tooling, preferably as standard equipment and built into the basic price, to give you the maximum flexibility and versatility and help your investment pay off many times over.*
6. *Quality must be important—the assurance that the machine supplied will retain its accuracy and performance for much longer than you need it to.*
7. *And reliability—certain knowledge that if your operator gums up the works, your supplier's service engineers will have you back in production FAST.*
8. *A technical back-up service to help you solve any really knotty machining problems, and comprehensive operator training if necessary, but at no extra cost.*
9. *And doubtless you would want to talk to a number of people who are already established customers of the supplier to establish how satisfied THEY are.*

Here is another example, this time for heating and ventilating equipment and which does not use a pre-printed check list but relies on the salesman listing down "Criteria" on his pad as it happens. This is the kind of "script" our sales managers should be constructing for their salesmen as an essential part of the continuous work we should be doing on developing their latent abilities and so keeping them happy to stay with UWC.

Establishing the Customer's Criteria for Ordering

At the very start of any sales presentation with a new potential customer, it is essential that the salesman establishes the main factors considered by the customer when he is trying to decide which of maybe several suppliers to choose.

Most customers faced with the need to make this kind of decision do not set about the decision making process scientifically. They often pick only one key factor from a particular supplier and play everything else by a kind of gut-feeling or from past experience. Thus, they often choose a supplier that has a worse all-round deal than they could have obtained had they done a better job of the decision-making process.

The salesman who is really on the ball helps the customer get through this process in the most positive way, by suggesting he lists down all his key factors and then compares each supplier against his list. In this way, the customer will be **absolutely sure** he makes the best decision, in respect of the best all-round deal for him and his company.

This is a completely logical suggestion for any salesman to make to any customer, and the best way for the salesman to actually **make** the suggestion is as follows:-

"Mr. Jones, we manufacture and install heating and ventilating equipment, and you are in the market (from time to time) for this kind of equipment. I'd like to be in with a chance of supplying you (on your next requirement), and I wonder, do you mind if I ask—when you're looking for a supplier of this kind of equipment, what are the key factors you consider when you choose—what is your Criteria for Ordering?"

Most times, after asking this question, the salesman will find that the customer starts talking—and most times he will say something about the price having to be right and the equipment having to do the job he wants done. Perhaps delivery may also be mentioned.

Then there will be a pause.

The salesman should then say to the customer: *"Do you mind if I get your list of criteria down on paper?"* and he writes down the key words relevant to what the customer has said so far.

These words might be:
PRICE
MUST DO THE JOB
DELIVERY

Then the salesman asks the customer some questions about these key words—questions like this:-

"On Price, Mr. Jones, do you tend to look for the lowest price, or are you more concerned with making sure you are getting the best all-round value for money—you know,

130

because of higher or lower running costs, or maintenance costs, and the life of the equipment, etc."

(Very rarely indeed will any customer say—"I **always** look for the lowest price".)

"When you say, 'must do the job', Mr. Jones, do you insist on your supplier adhering rigidly to your specification or to the ideas you already have, or do you look to the supplier to come up with better ways of doing the job, or less expensive ways of achieving the same, or better, results?"

(Again, few customers will admit that they **always** consider they know best.)

"On Delivery, Mr. Jones, considering the kind of equipment we are talking about, isn't it usually a case of the supplier being able to deliver according to when you want to start installation? In order words, he has to match in with your schedules, rather than supply, sort of 'off the shelf'."

After this session of questions, the salesman will have added words to his initial list of the customer's criteria—probably words like this:-

PRICE—best value for money.

MUST DO THE JOB—or be a better, simpler, less expensive way of getting the same or better results.

DELIVERY—needs to dovetail into customer's schedules, or able to install the equipment at the most convenient time to the customer.

Now the salesman sets out to complete the rest of the customer's criteria for ordering list. He asks another question:-

"Okay, Mr. Jones, we've got Price, Spec. and Delivery down. But there must be quite a few other factors you consider. Can I get these down too?"

Here is where the salesman will be able to give the customer a lot of help (but gently) and at the same time build up a list of criteria for the customer that gives us a much better chance of getting the business.

Most customers may frown and say nothing after the salesman has asked that last question. Others may splutter a little in hesitation. Others may say, "What have you got in mind?" Whichever; after about four seconds, the salesman can offer a few suggestions:-

"Well, how about Reliability and Longest possible operating Life, Mr. Jones? Isn't that a significant factor for you? Specification and performance is important, yes, but you want equipment which will perform to spec. for umpteen years without problems, don't you?"

Of course he does. So down "Reliability and Longest Life" goes on the list.

"Do you do your own design work, and handle the liaison with the sub-contractors who do the duct work, etc? Or do you look for a supplier who can take all this work off your hands and look after the whole job, give or take the electric wiring and a few specialist things like that? And one who can guarantee the satisfactory functioning of the whole system."

This is where the salesman finds out whether the customer has his own design staff, or whether our ability to handle most of the "contract management" business will play a major role in justifying a higher price for the equipment.

Okay, if he has his own design team, we know the salesman has a harder job on his hands. But fortunately, few customers have this facility. Most really need our overall package deal. So the salesman gets another criterion down on the list. "Able to Provide a Complete Package Deal", or "Able to Look After all Contract Liaison and Design", or "Total Guaranteed Package".

"How about 'Lowest Running Costs' and 'Lowest Maintenance Costs', Mr. Jones?" No problem—every customer will say Yes.

"And what about Space? Do you look for equipment—or a design for the installation—which will take up the very minimum of your valuable, and expensive, factory (or office) space?"

"Are Labour Relations important to you, Mr. Jones? With the Health and Safety at Work Act and all this campaigning for a better working environment, what kind of part does this play in your decisions on equipment of this nature?"

Perhaps our 75 years of experience and stability can be added, linking reputation to spares and service like this:-

"What about the risk of your supplier going broke half-way

through the job, Mr. Jones? There are a lot of cowboys and one-man-bands in this business, as well as quite a few long-established, reputable and stable companies with properly set up spares and service organisations—like us. Is stability, reputation and the spares/service aspect important to you?"

(You may have a chance to mention our £2 million of spares always in stock at HQ, as well as the "75 years in business" bit).

And when there are no more tangible factors to suggest, the salesman can play his two intangible "aces":-

"How important to you is Communications, Mr. Jones? What I mean is, the ability to contact a supplier quickly and easily, get through to the person you want, have your requirements interpreted correctly, and acted upon, and all that kind of thing? Thinking back over the past few weeks, how many times have you come up against problems when you've tried to get in touch with your suppliers?"

(He'll think of some. Everyone has problems).

"We work very hard at getting this right. We're very careful about the people we employ who have contact with our customers. We've got less of a problem communicating between departments, too, because all our engineers, like me, are capable of looking after all the aspects of any job. If you reckon Communication is important enough, Mr. Jones, I'll write it down. If you aren't too bothered, fair enough."

(But the salesman has already made his point, hasn't he?)

"Finally, Mr. Jones, what about Philosophy? How important to you is having a supplier with the right Philosophy? What I mean is; is the supplier a 'Product Orientated' company or a 'Customer Orientated' company? Is he mainly interested in selling fan units, or cyclones, or is he mainly interested in providing the best installation to solve a customer's problems and achieve his objectives? Does he firmly believe that it is the customer who pays all the wages, or has he lost sight of the basic fact?"

"We believe the customer is the most important person in our business."

So if all goes well, the salesman should finish up with a

complete "Criteria for Ordering" list for the customer which looks like this:-

PRICE — best value for money.

SPECIFICATION — must do the job, or be a better, simpler, less expensive way of getting the same or better results.

DELIVERY — must be able to meet customer's schedules.

RELIABILITY/ LONGEST LIFE — must give good service well past depreciation period (find out what this is).

DESIGN/ CONTRACTING — must be able to handle nearly everything.

RUNNING COSTS — must be lowest.

MAINTENANCE COSTS — must be lowest.

SPACE — must take up the smallest space.

LABOUR RELATIONS — seeks to improve them (or meet requirements of the Health and Safety at Work Act).

STABILITY/SPARES/ SERVICE — won't go bust half-way through the job.

COMMUNICATIONS — easy to do business with.

PHILOSOPHY — puts the customer first.

Having established the customer's Criteria for Ordering, the salesman can then go on and either:-

1. Prove to the customer that we can meet his criteria on all points—having done so, get agreement from the customer that we will be included in any list of suppliers which are asked to quote for future work.

or

2. Ask the customer which other suppliers he uses, and suggest that these suppliers are compared with us against the Criteria for Ordering list. (Salesman draws vertical columns on his pad to the right of the criteria list, one column for each supplier, putting us on the far left column, and discussing us **FIRST**—just in case the customer runs out of time).

After this, the final questions should always be either:-

1. "When do you expect the next job will be?"
   "When would you like me to call, then?"
   "What else would you like me to do, or show you now?"
   "Will there be anyone else I should talk to?"

or

2. (If there is already a specific requirement)
   "If you are happy that we are a good supplier then, Mr. Jones, can we get down to looking at your specific requirements? Can we have a look at the site? What have you done about it so far? Have you received any quotes yet? Can I have a look at the Spec.—it will save us some time if I can see what other firms are suggesting you do?" (not forgetting to "SHUT UP" after each question, of course).

NOTE:- ALWAYS LEAVE THE CRITERIA FOR ORDERING LIST WITH THE CUSTOMER WHEN LEAVING—(so it is best to take a carbon copy when writing the list).

ACTION Each salesman should re-write this set of notes, using the syle and words he would use when face to face with a new customer.

When satisfied—write it out another six times—this way, it will become fairly firmly fixed in the mind. Then use it, and see what happens. It may not work every time, but don't give up if the first time it flops. It may only work partially—okay,

135

use the parts you succeed in getting down to.

Practice makes perfect--and nothing is perfect in selling.

The Technology Barrier

Most of our salesmen are engineers or technologists of some kind. Only in our consumer divisions is this not so. And the problem of having a technical guy doing the selling for us is that he spends 99% of his time spouting technical data about our products and discussing technical problems with our customers, and completely loses sight of the commercial considerations of why he's got himself face-to-face with the customer in the first place.

Our salesmen aren't paid to solve problems, they are paid to get orders. If they get an order by solving a problem, fine, as long as we still make a profit from the job.

Our salesmen don't ask anything like enough questions—and the questions they do ask aren't commercial questions. Here are a few examples which would warrant distribution to all our sales personnel:

"What is this problem costing you?"

"How are you thinking of solving it?"

"What would happen if you did nothing?"

"Who else apart from you is involved in this problem—or in finding a solution to it?"

"How much money has been allocated to solving this problem?"

"How did you reach this particular figure?"

"When will this money be available?"

"If we can produce a significantly better answer for slightly more than your budget figure, would you look at it?"

Then don't forget we need to find out what competition we are up against, and that competition's strengths and weaknesses:-

"Which other suppliers are you discussing this problem with?"

"Who decides which supplier gets the order?"

"When are the other quotations due?"

"Have you used any of these suppliers before?"

"Which supplier do you favour at this stage?"

"Why?"

Do you all see the point?

136

Give a man a fish and you feed him for a day.

Teach a man how to fish and you feed him for life.

23—TRAINING IN MONEY MATTERS

Your personal estimate of the percentage improvement possible.

Prices	Variable Costs
Sales (10%)	Fixed Costs

The figure in brackets is our management consultant's estimate of the probable percentage improvement in a business where technology is paramount and the salesforce is highly engineering orientated.

Use this space for notes and calculations.

24—COMPANY PROFILES

Our management consultant doesn't feel we are projecting our corporate image very well to our customers—especially large potential customers and especially on our export side.

He says we have no literature available other than product sales literature—nothing which gives a complete picture of Universal Widgets total capability to supply the larger customer consistently, reliably and over a long period.

He's right, we haven't. So here is an example of an inexpensive "Company Profile" document which we could follow to very good effect when we go after those larger contracts. The Photographs and literature which go with this kind of document we can easily find.

You can see how simple it would be to get translations done for any country in the world. If this particular kind of document is in the right language, we stand a much better chance of getting away with the rest of the package being in English.

Profile of THE BANRO GROUP

The Banro Group is made up of six direct subsidiary manufacturing companies in the UK and, following the acquisition of a majority interest in Farnier & Penin, a leading French transport component manufacturer, it has gained its first major foothold in Europe, controlled through Edward Rose (France) Ltd., a wholly owned subsidiary of the Group.

Each company has its own manufacturing plant and in the UK four of these plants are situated in the West Midlands, one at Telford, Shropshire and one at High Wycombe in Buckinghamshire. In France the plant is situated at Bressuire, between Nantes and Poitiers. The individual member companies continuously utilise the technical expertise and manufacturing facilities provided by their sister companies to mutually create products of the highest technical excellence.

The principal activities of the Banro Group are the manufacture of framed windows, rolled sections, pressings, motor car body components, off highway vehicle components, the continuous plating of metal in coil form and electro plating applications, all for the sea, air, road, rail, domestic appliance and building industries.

One of the most actively creative engineering groups in its field, Banro has an excellent export record, selling services and technical expertise—as well as products— throughout Europe, Scandinavia and Africa. A measure of the Group's stature in overseas markets is that they have negotiated and obtained technical aid licence agreements in such important developing market areas as the Middle East and South East Asia.

Group Company Structure and Financial Status

Banro Consolidated Industries Ltd

Address: Pelsall Road,
                Brownhills, Walsall
                West Midlands WS8 7HP
                England

The Group comprises:
William Bate Limited
Plated Strip (International) Limited
* Pertectinite Limited
Edward Rose (Birmingham) Limited
Edward Rose (Telford) Limited
Edward Rose (Sections) Limited
Edward Rose (France) Limited
* Etablissements Farnier & Penin S.A.
Edward Rose (Plastics) Limited
* Pertectinite Limited is a subsidiary of William Bate Limited.
* Etablissements Farnier & Penin S.A. is a subsidiary of Edward Rose (France) Limited.

Associated Companies

Edward Rose (Manufacturing) USA Inc
Banro Consolidated Industries Limited is a quoted Company on the London and Provincial Stock Exchanges.

Financial Status

The financial status of the Group is very strong. A high proportion of the net profits have been retained in the business.

140

The main figures for the Banro Consolidated Industries Limited Group of Companies are:-

	Profit Before Taxation	Capital Employed
1979	£1,156,646	£6,031,603
1978	£1,074,328	£4,351,687
1977	£ 911,502	£3,807,794
1976	£ 651,335	£3,368,580

The turnover in 1979 was £15,784,402 of which £1,239,256 was the value of goods exported. The average number of employees in 1979 was 928. This number has now risen to approximately 1,200.

Management Structure of Banro Group

Edward Rose	Chairman and Chief Executive
Denis Richard Greenhough	Deputy Chairman
William John Hooper, F.C.A.	Finance Director
Ronald Francis Bate	
Peter Lewis Andrews	
Alan Victor Pitcher	

The bankers of Banro are:
The Midland Bank Limited
The Bridge
Walsall
West Midlands
England.

A copy of the published Annual Report and Accounts will be supplied on request to a prospective customer.

Principal Products and Services

The principal products and services supplied to customers by the Group are described under each Company heading in this document.

Business and Marketing Objectives

These are briefly:

Product supremacy and market leadership.

Steady and stable long term growth of the Group.

Creation of a fully European orientated Group.

141

Achievement of a satisfactory return on the capital invested in the Group.

Market diversification without diversification of basic production facilities or technology.

The Group recognises the inter-dependence which exists between the motor and other prime manufacturers and their specialist suppliers such as Banro. Because of this its management policies are primarily aimed at the maintenance and further development of high commercial, quality, production and delivery disciplines and standards of performance.

These objectives require for their achievement the total involvement and personal commitment of every member of the management team and good labour relations at all levels in the organisation.

New Business Required

The series manufacture of customer designed motor component and other products of the type already manufactured by the Group.

The series manufacture of any other type of product which required the same production facilities and technology that already exists within the Group.

This includes window assemblies and decorative or functional fittings to aircraft, radios, television, agricultural equipment and domestic appliances.

Licences to manufacture proprietary products which are compatible to the existing range of products.

Quality Assurance and Product Support Services

The Group maintains a Quality Assurance organization which includes inspection and control of its producers and suppliers on similar lines to that applied to Edward Rose by its main customers.

Product support includes:

Assistance to customers in product development.

A Value Analysis service which aims to improve quality and functional integrity and also to reduce manufacturing costs.

Environmental, wear and life testing of products in liaison with customers.

UK Banro Group Companies and Management Structure
William Bate Limited
Directors:
A V Pitcher (Chairman); M H Flavell (Director & General Manager); Edward Rose; G F Bate; R F Bate; J M Bate; T W Smithson; W J Hooper FCA; D G Blagden.
Address:
William Bate Limited
Hospital Street
Walsall
West Midlands
WS2 8QQ   Tel: Walsall (0922) 21232
England

Founded nearly 100 years ago, the Company specialises in almost every form of metal finishing on a large scale and is a major contract metal finisher in Europe, having a capacity of over 800 tons per week of electro plating and general metal finishing for the automotive, building, engineering, domestic appliance, electrical, furniture and hardware industries.

The wide range of finishes available include bright chrome on steel, zinc diecasting and plastics, black chrome, in addition nickel, zinc, paint, anodising, electroless nickel, and a wide range of antique finishes together with copper, lead and brass. Polishing facilities, both hand and automatic are available.

The Company designs and makes its own jigs and has designed and built much of its own plant. Over ninety years of experience goes into each finish offered and quality is assured by the Company's expert technicians, carefully regulated automatic plant and fully equipped laboratory testing facilities.

Plated Strip (International) Limited
Directors:
D R Greenhough (Chairman and Managing); K Andrews; Edward Rose
Executive Directors:
B K Johnson; G W Cooper.
Address:
Plated Strip (International) Limited
Wharfdale Road
Tyseley

Birmingham
B11 2DL
England

Tel: 021 706 1186-7-8
Telex: 337875

Specialises in supplying pre-plated coiled steel to customers own specification. The Company is unique in the UK in being able to undertake these highly specialised processes, with exports to over 21 countries accounting for a high volume of total production.

The plant has continuous strip plating lines for chrome, nickel, brass and copper finishes. There is also plant for hot tinning steel and non-ferrous strip in coil, with finished products being extensively used in the stationery, luggage, electronic, domestic equipment and builders hardware industries.

Edward Rose (Birmingham) Limited

Directors:

Edward Rose (Chairman and Managing); W J Hooper FCA (Deputy Chairman and Finance); A V Pitcher (Plant Operations); J K Anderson (Sales); A C Louis (Works).

Address:

Edward Rose (Birmingham) Limited
Edrose Works
Pelsall Road
Brownhills Walsall
West Midlands WS8 7HP
England

Tel: Brownhills 5100
Telex: 339870 Edrose

The Edward Rose (Birmingham) Limited factory is conveniently located in a light industrial area just North of Birmingham and close to both Walsall and Wolverhampton. It has easy access to a wide range of specialist lower tier suppliers and all the technical facilities required by a leading component manufacturer.

The factory has 100,000 sq ft of high grade covered space, which is well sited in 4¼ acres of land which is suitable for further factory development.

The largest turnover unit in the Banro Group, the Company —which in 1980 celebrates its 25th anniversary— specialises in the manufacture of framed windows assemblies, bumpers and manipulated cold rolled sections for passenger cars, commer-

144

cial and off highway vehicles. Founded in 1955, the Company possesses highly sophisticated production machinery and a quarter of century of expertise in the forming of metal into any shape and size in accordance with customers' specification and requirements. A feature of the production processes are the in-process gauges which guarantee that every part precisely meets specification. The quality of paint finish is ensured by the recent installation of a new automatic cathodic electro deposition paint plant, coupled with powder coating paint facilities.

The production of complete window units is undertaken from the making of frames through all the processes of assembling rubber mouldings and glass, including fitting hinge and fastening mechanisms. There are many finishes for such typical items as sliding windows for vans, opening tailgates, quarterlights, opening rear lights, bumpers for cars and hinged windows for agricultural and commercial vehicles.

Edward Rose (Telford) Limited
Directors:
Edward Rose (Chairman); W J Hooper FCA (Deputy Chairman & Finance); A V Pitcher (Managing); N W Owen (Works); J K Anderson (Sales); D R Greenhough; K Andrews.
Address
Edward Rose (Telford) Limited
Tweedale Industrial Estate
Telford
Salop
TF7 4JP   Tel: Telford 586521
England

The Company is equipped with modern power presses ranging from 10 tonnes to 250 tonnes and also has extensive follow on operations including welding, spot welding and assembly. These facilities are applied on products for the automative and domestic appliance industries using aluminium, stainless steel, mild steel, electro plated steel and p.v.c. coated materials.

The wide diversity of products ranges from reflective trims for gas fires, steel panels for electric space heaters, to automotive treadplates, wheel trims, parcel shelves, instrument

145

panels, head restraints and bumpers.

Edward Rose (Sections) Limited

Directors:

Edward Rose (Chairman); W J Hooper FCA (Deputy Chairman & Finance); P J Hollis (Managing); A V Pitcher.

Address:

Edward Rose (Sections) Limited
186 Pelsall Road
Brownhills Walsall
West Midlands   Tel: Brownhills 5100
WS8 7HP   Telex: 339870 Edrose
England

Edward Rose (Sections) Limited produces cold rolled sections for other Group subsidiaries and many external customers on the building, domestic appliance, electrical, air conditioning and other service industries.

The recent development within the Company has been the manufacture of close formed lock seam tube for the roller blind industry.

High level of output and quality is obtained from continuous operation, rolling machines and the size and flexibility of the plant enables the Company to offer medium or large volume production for sections which customers require in the materials they specify. The Company is now in a position to handle strip up to 470 mm wide by 5 mm thick in lengths up to 6 metres.

Edward Rose (Plastics) Limited

Directors:

Edward Rose (Chairman); W R Richardson (Managing); W J Hooper FCA (Finance & Secretary); J K Anderson (Sales); R R Hearn (Technical); J R Sparks.

Address:

Edward Rose (Plastics) Limited
Micropost Building
Lincoln Road
Cressex Industrial Estate
High Wycombe Bucks
HP12 3RA   Tel: (0494) 25049
England

146

Edward Rose (Plastics) Limited specialises in the manufacture of precision profiles in high performance plastic materials.

These profiles, together with those incoporating laminates, can be extended by the addition of metal substrates, or inclusions, based on the technology of the other companies within the Banro Group.

Edward Rose (Plastics) Limited is fully equipped with modern extruders with compatible custom built down stream equipment designed for accurate calibration and finishing.

In-house die design, development manufacture and a full quality control procedure completes a comprehensive service to all branches of industry.

For the Automotive Industry products include: body side mouldings/trim; bumper pads; profile extrusions for carpet retainers; drip rail finishers—both bright rail and black—windscreen finishers; tread plates and other profile extrusions—including overflow pipes and windscreen washer pipes.

For the Domestic Appliance/Electrical Industries the Company produces rigid and flexible profile extrusions, fridge shelf finishes and working surrounds for the tops of domestic appliances.

For the Lighting Industry the Company produces rigid profiles for light tracking and this is seen as a potentially important growth market area.

For the home markets (although they would still be highly relevant in export markets) we would also gain advantages over our competitors if we were to use what is called a "Supplier Evaluation" report and some letters from our customers saying how pleased they are with our products and service.

Supplier Evaluation is a technique used by quite a few major firms before their purchasing departments chose new suppliers. They want the answers to lots of questions before they'll even consider buying anything from the company being examined. The average company that receives a Supplier Evaluation form for the first time, out of the blue, doesn't know what to do with it, makes a hash of it and so loses any chance it had of getting the business.

Many companies refuse to fill in such a form, feeling that

147

the information requested is private and confidential and that the potential customer should mind his own bloody business. Incredible. If you check the example I've provided of such a Supplier Evaluation document (see pages 149-152) ask yourself how much of the information asked for could be obtained from a couple of telephone calls and a search at Companies House for annual reports and accounts.

If UWC prepared its own Supplier Evaluation report, and used it religiously in every selling situation—BEFORE being asked for it, we must gain a significant edge over our competitors AND boost our own corporate identity.

If we backed this up with some real life letters from customers, like those on pages 153 and 154, I reckon half the resistance our salesmen get from cautious potential customers would disappear.

Finally, our machine tool salesforce would benefit from using a printed sheet like the example, on page 155, which paints a clear-cut picture of why someone should buy from us. This kind of sheet should be included in every quotation, along with the letters and the Supplier Evaluation report. (Use the standard Institute of Purchasing Management form—the IPM gives us extra credibility.)

Get to it........!

THE INSTITUTE OF PURCHASING MANAGEMENT
SUPPLIER EVALUATION REPORT

Supplier:

Contract: Date:

Reasons for asking for all this information

When suppliers have to fulfil contracts over a lengthy period, customers must be certain that there is negligible risk of the suppliers going broke; that suppliers do not become over-dependant on one customer and can finance the cost of producing to the customer's schedules and also finance expansion of facilities if this is necessary. A supplier's plans for growth need to dovetail closely into a customer's plans for increasing his business with that supplier. Pricing policies must demonstrate a supplier's awareness of the need for profit, rather than be based on initial marginal costings designed to secure a contract, with higher prices to follow.

All these things the professional purchasing executive must establish before orders are placed. The questions that follow in this Supplier Evaluation document are designed to establish these facts. Please answer all questions accurately; there is no future for the relationship between customer and supplier if a false picture is presented at the very beginning of the relationship.

THE COMPANY

Full Name:

Registered Office:

Headquarters:

How long in present business?

Spares and Service Depots and Sales Offices: (give all addresses)

OWNERSHIP

Type of Company — Private or Public:

Directors:

Shareholders: (majority holding first)

Subsidiary interests: (or other divisions)
(if group, please draw family tree).

continue on separate sheet if necessary.

MANAGEMENT

Please list names and extent of experience of those executives relevant to this contract and to general customer relations.

FINANCIAL

Please provide last Annual Report and Chairman's Statement if this is available, or Company Profile literature.

Last 3 years performance:	Turnover	Profit	Return on Capital	Gearing Ratio
198				
198				
198				

Next 5 years projection of turnover: (excluding price increases)

Terms of Payment:

Quantity Discount Structure:

150

FACILITIES

Does the Company manufacture, assemble or distribute its products? (those applicable to the contract).

If it assembles or distributes, where are the products manufactured?

      Country of Origin:

      Name of Manufacturer:

		NOW	3 YEARS AGO
Number of employees:	production:	....	....
	administration:	....	....
	sales force:	....	....
	service force:	....	....

Nature of production equipment:

Nature of accounting and administrative equipment/systems:

If you use a computer, which kind and for what?

Quality Assurance, testing and inspection facilities:

Government, Ministry of Defence or other Approvals:

MARKETS AND CUSTOMERS

What proportion of your total turnover comes from the products you are quoting for on this contract?

How do you see this proportion changing over the next 5 years?

From what kind of companies/industries does most of this business come?

Please give the names, addresses, telephone numbers and contacts of 3 current customers whom we can contact to ask about the service they get from you and the reliability of your products.

Further copies of this Supplier Evaluation document can be obtained from the Institute of Purchasing Management, Concorde House, 24 Warwick New Road, Royal Leamington Spa, Warwickshire CV32 5JH, price 27p each incl. VAT. All orders should be accompanied by remittance.

HARRISON & SONS (LONDON) LIMITED

A Member of the Harrison Group

Printing House Lane
Hayes Middlesex
UB3 1HQ England
Telephone 01 573 3828
Telex 23744

Directors
R T H Harrison MA Chairman
R A Boxall Managing Director
B L Hibbitt
K F H Leathers ACMA
D S Robinson

Registered Office
Harrison House Coates Lane
High Wycombe Buckinghamshire
HP13 5EZ England
Registered Number
882698 England

Mr. Peter Bosworth
Managing Director
Sales Control and Record Systems Limited
Concorde House
24 Warwick New Road
Royal Leamington Spa
CV32 5JH

13 June 1979

Dear Peter

For a long time it has been my intention to write and tell you
how valuable I find the sales recording and control system you
and John Fenton put together for our commercial colour printing
sales force.

The system is extremely useful in helping salesmen to organise
all the various things they are doing into a formal method of
working.

Properly used, the system painlessly compels salesmen to perform
in a superior professional manner.

On day-to-day affairs in dealing with your Company I must give
high praise to your sales administration manager, Mrs. Joy Strang.
Her help and advice has been invaluable to me at all times and I
am grateful for the back-up service which Joy provides.

Yours sincerely

Fred Pamphilion

Fred Pamphilion
Graphic Design and Print Sales

153

Barbecco Limited

Sales Office and Showroom
28a Devonshire Street
London W1N 1RF

Distributors, Import/Export

Telephone 01-935 6800

Head Office and Showroom
Goldwell House
Bath Road
Newbury RG13 1JH
Berkshire/England
Sales   (0635) 30301
General   (0635) 30373

Reg. Office: Champness Cowper & Co

Reg. Company No 114 2146, London

Mrs. J.M. Strang
Sales Administration Manager
SCRS Ltd.
Concorde House
24 Warwick New Road
Royal Leamington Spa
Warwickshire CV32 5JH

XXXXX   Newbury, 23.3.1979
our ref: MB/DG
your ref:

Dear Mrs. Strang,

We recently asked you to send us new refill sets for
our Sales Control and Record Systems and we would
like to use the opportunity to inform you that we have
found the system a great improvement in the control of
sales and record keeping with our salesmen. We feel
that the real benefit will come in the second year of use
as we shall be able to use comparison figures and
statistics recorded with the system during the previous
year.

We wish you every success for your system in the future.

Yours sincerely,
BARBECCO LIMITED

M. Beckers
Director

154

UWC Machine Tool Division
Sample Page for Proposal Document
Here are a number of key factors which anyone contemplating the purchase of a new machine tool must weigh up, when assessing the possible supplier of that machine tool:-

Quality
UWC guarantees the quality of its equipment—not just in terms of holding accuracy and performance over a very long working life, but also in terms of efficiency—the most production, the least down time, the easiest programming, on-the-spot-editing, etc. UWC pioneered Computerised Numerical Controlled Widget Crushing, and is still well ahead of the field.

Reliability
With UWC, you have a machine and a control system designed and built for each other, and both by UWC. Thus, not only does the total package perform at the optimum, all your servicing is handled by one team. And if your operator has a bad day and gums up the works, UWC's team of engineers will have you back in production—**FAST**.

Proven Performance
There are more than 1000 UWC machines and control systems in use throughout the world, and over 600 are within the UK. This means that no UWC customer will ever need to play 'guinea pig'. Instead, he will install a machine and control system that has been production proved a thousand times over.

Most new customers want to talk to other UWC customers about their experience with the machines and the control systems. This our salesmen are always happy to arrange.

Training
Even though the CNC control unit is so much simpler than NC type systems, UWC provide all the training a customer requires, for operator, setter and programmer—free.

Back-up
UWC is a sound, profitable, British-based group. Its extensive research and development facilities, world-wide group technology and thousand-plus customers mean that UWC's technical back-up is second to none. If it's crushable, a UWC machine has crushed it. So if you hit a really knotty pro-

duction problem UWC's back-up team should be able to find the answer.

Financial Aid

We've left the crunch factor till last—where do you find the money to invest in a UWC Widget Crusher and CNC control system? UWC has long realised that spare capital is not the most prolific of assets. So the company has set out to be as helpful as it can in finding the necessary funds for its customers. UWC does not operate its own hire purchase division, it simply maintains a close working relationship with the leading finance houses in the UK, and this leads to its customers being offered the keenest interest rates around.

Six good reasons why your supplier should be UWC.

24–COMPANY PROFILES

Your personal estimate of the percentage improvement possible.

Prices	Variable Costs
Sales	Fixed Costs
(10%)	

The figure in brackets is our management consultant's estimate of the probable percentage improvement in a business where only sales literature designed by the company's engineers is used. i.e. all technical, nothing commercial.

Use this space for notes, calculations and drafting profiles.

25–CONVERTING MORE QUOTATIONS INTO ORDERS

Our average conversion ration of quotations to orders is probably about 5 to 1. In other words, for every 5 quotations we submit, we win one order. Not bad in our business.

But what if our ratio could be reduced to 3 to 1? For the same number of quotations, we would win 40% more orders. All other things being equal, that means a 40% increase in sales.

How do we reduce our conversion ratio? Well, first we do ourselves what our own buyers are going to do with our suppliers. Check back on "Purchasing Policies" and you'll see what I mean.

That, I am told, will take at least six months. Formats of quotations have to be changed. Habits of a lifetime have to go out of the window.

But for a possible 40% increase in sales—isn't it going to be worth it?

According to our management consultant, wherever he goes in the world, he finds the same thing; companies sending out quotations which look more like invoices. Companies quoting legal and semi-legal jargon to people who haven't even said, "Yes, we'll buy it". He firmly believes that 90% of the business which companies like us chase but lose to our competitors or to budget delays and cancellations, is lost because of the nature of the quotation—that piece of paper which is supposed to confirm all the key points discussed by the salesman, but which never does.

The quotation is all the ammunition we give the key contact in a customer company, with which he often has to sell the idea to his own board of directors. He hasn't the benefit of our sales training programme, our salesmen's intimate product knowledge, or our salesmen's elaborate visual aids and other selling tools. He only devotes a small fraction of his time to thinking about our product and our competitors' offers.

The whole deal may be of only minor importance to him, compared with all his other problems.

So what kind of a selling job is that guy going to do for us?

The least we can do is provide him with the best kind of ammunition; and his board of directors will only be interested in one thing—how much is the deal going to make or save them, over what kind of time; plus, can they afford it.

25–CONVERTING MORE QUOTATIONS INTO ORDERS

Your personal estimate of the percentage improvement possible.

Prices	Variable Costs
Sales	Fixed Costs
(10%)	

The figure in brackets is our management consultant's estimate of the probable percentage improvement in a business where the quotations all look like invoices and only contain Specification, Delivery, Price and Terms of Business. Okay, the text mentions that 40% improvement is possible, but this is only achieved when **everyone** *gets cracking with total enthusiasm and dedication to changing the format; salesforce (who have to obtain a lot more and a lot different information from the customer), sales office (who have to produce the quotations) and management (who have to firmly believe it's all worth the time and trouble). Usually, after the first euphoric 2-3 months, it all slides back to how it was before, so the project is never given enough time to prove itself. The companies most successful at presenting true 'proposals', rather than quotations, get conversion ratios of around 2 to 1.* **They** *feel it is worth the time and trouble.*

Use this space for notes and calculations.

26–TELEX CLOSING

Our salesmen don't have time to follow up every quotation we issue to customers and prospective customers. Thus, a lot of the small fish escape our net, and some of the bigger fish.

Telephoning customers to ask if our quotation has been considered and if any decision has been made is not effective and never will be.

But Telex is.

So when you have a situation where you know when the customer quoted wants to have delivery, or installation, use your Telex to close the sale.

Here is an example:-

REF. OUR QUOTATION 4XY/7AR DATED JAN. 17th FOR WIDGETS GRADE B.

IMPERATIVE WE HAVE YOUR ORDER NUMBER BY WEDNESDAY THIS WEEK IF WE ARE TO MEET YOUR DELIVERY DATE OF MARCH 10th.

PLEASE CAN YOU TELEX OR TELEPHONE ORDER NUMBER SO THAT OUT PRODUCTION DEPT. CAN PROCEED.

UNIVERSAL WIDGET CORPORATION
J. B. STANLEY.

It works. It really does. I've seen it.

26–TELEX CLOSING
Your personal estimate of the percentage improvement possible.

Prices	Variable Costs
Sales	**Fixed Costs**
(2%)	(1%)

The figures in brackets are our management consultant's estimate of the probable percentage in a business where the constraints on time make personal following up quotations an impossibility except for big jobs.

Use this space for notes and calculations.

There's never time to do it right but always time to do it again.

27–SALESFORCE CONTROL

Our Salesmen are successful—right across the group.

What I mean by that is they are achieving the sales turnover we are setting for them, and keeping selling costs within our budgets.

But our management consultant tells me that we could do much better, with no more salesmen, by steadily improving the performance of the salesmen we now employ. He also says that by doing this, we will lose less salesmen.

Worse to come. According to our consultant, our field sales managers spend far too much time on paperwork, and far too little time out in the field with their salesmen. We do not know in sufficient detail the true personal performance of each of our salesmen, and because of this lack of data, we are failing to do all the things that **can** be done to improve our selling performance.

Our management consultant suggests a radical change in the reporting and control systems paperwork used by our various sales forces. He recommends we look closely at a proprietary system for full sales force control known as SCRS, which, he says, reduces paperwork for both salesman and manager as well as providing all the detailed performance data necessary for sales management to continually improve results.

There is a comprehensive book available on this SCRS sales force control system. Please obtain a copy and learn what this system might do to help us. You can get it, price £4 from Sales Control and Record Systems Limited, Concorde House, 24 Warwick New Road, Royal Leamington Spa, CV32 5JH, Warwickshire, England. Meanwhile, here is an extract:

(I know I said that in carrying out this Action Plan there would be little or no need to actually SPEND more money, okay, SCRS would be an exception—but a legitimate one, because if your case for sales force control is sound, this system will pay for itself from increased sales in about one

month. Thus, the board will undoubtedly look favourably on any request for expenditure in this area.)

The world is full of companies that use salesmen to bring their products or services to the market place or to the end consumer.

For each and every one, an efficient and effective salesforce control system is essential.

Accepting that such a control system will not solve ALL the problems a company will have when it strives to look ahead and see where it is likely to be in one, two, five or even ten years time, the right system, starting as it does at the company's "spearhead", *WILL* provide production, finance, research and development, advertising, after sales service, corporate planning, the main board of directors, or the managing director himself, with more than enough information to enable these divisions to do their own sums with much more accuracy and confidence.

At the same time, of course, the right system of salesforce control will ensure that the company is selling to maximum effect, both on volume and on profitability, and at minimum cost.

No company that wants to still be in business in ten years time, and especially if it wants to be bigger by then, or much more profitable by then, can afford to ignore this important part of its activites.

This extract concerns itself with but one system for salesforce control. It has been developed over more than thirteen years of continual work, first by the Institution of Sales Engineers, then by the Institute of Sales Management, and since 1969 by the training and management consultancy division of ISE and ISM, Structured Training Limited. More than 15,000 salesmen and sales managers have contributed to the system's development, and in its standard form, known as SCRS, the system is currently being used very successfully by well over 1500 companies.

In addition to the key objectives already mentioned, the SCRS system has been designed to cope effectively with two of the most onerous problems every company employing salesmen has to live with.

1. **Salesmen hate paperwork**

   SCRS reduces the salesman's paperwork to a practical minimum, and quickly makes the salesman see for himself that the paperwork he has to handle is not only valuable to him and his company—it actually makes his job easier to do successfully.

2. **Sales Managers never have time to process paperwork properly**

   SCRS processes the manager's paperwork semi-automatically. For a salesforce of ten salesmen, he would be involved for no more than one hour per week. And he would probably be getting five or six times as much usable data from the system and absolutely no waffle.

Market Penetration

SCRS's main objective is to achieve maximum market at minimum cost. The system makes significant contributions to longer term planning in respect of market development and product development, as the reader will see later in this book, but the key area is in getting the most out of existing markets with the existing products.

Companies that are some way from market saturation, or that have many competitors, or both, can expect to five-fold turnover in four years with little or no increase in the number of salesmen employed, if they use SCRS fully and their salesforce accepts the system with no reservations or deliberate obstruction.

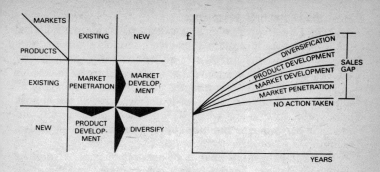

Strategy for Profitable Growth

The normal concept is for the company to maximise on market penetration as a first priority, then moving into market development (new markets for the existing products) as phase two, followed by product development (new products for existing markets) as phase three and finally diversification (new products for new markets) as phase four. However, many companies successfully tackle all phases at the same time if resources are adequate. Others short-cut the established concepts and go for diversification by acquisition (taking over other companies), seeing this as a more cost effective method than doing their own market and product development. (Only one in ten new products developed ever successfully reach the market place.)

167

Measuring Current Performance

IF THE PERFORMANCE of a salesman is judged solely on the turnover he produces in a given period of time, it will always be infernally difficult to either control his activities or effect any measurable improvement in his performance.

Likewise, if the performance of the whole company is judged solely on the turnover it achieves, it will be almost impossible to pin-point specific problem areas which are reducing performance and take appropriate—and fast—remedial action.

Measuring the performance of a salesman, and of a company's whole sales operation, is a task needing to be done day by day, week by week, month by month, continuously throughout the year. The measurements taken need to be much more specific and detailed than just an overall figure for turnover.

Many companies spend thousands of hours a year keeping tabs on this kind of thing. Paperwork and statistics lord over everything and everyone. Very soon the key people become infuriated with the vast amount of administration required. De-motivation and falling performance logically follow.

So the wrong kind of measurement system can easily defeat the whole object, which is to show the company where it is now, and where each of its salesmen are now—and to point the way in finite and practical terms to where both company and salesmen will be this time next quarter, or next year. Then the company's target can be related to this prediction, and the amount of improvement needed in individual and corporate performance can be calculated, without which the company's target will simply *not* be achieved.

The right kind of measurement system will make the salesman's task easier, not harder, and will involve the sales manager (or his delegated subordinate) in no more than one hour a week of analysis time. The sales manager also has at his finger-tips at all times those figures which the managing director invariably hollers for in the middle of every board meeting. No more instant panics and red faces.

SCRS provides a system of performance measurement which is as simple as possible, gives the most comprehensive

168

information in both numerical and ratio form, and fits, with little or no modifications, practically every company situation we have subsequently come across.

This is how it works.......

Stage One—Weekly Call Analysis

Each week, every salesman submits to H.Q. a list of all the calls he has made during the week, and what happened on each call.

The list is written on a specially designed A4 size form, entitled "Call Analysis", see fig. A. Writing is reduced to a minimum, the salesman only has to enter the name of each customer in longhand, the rest of the recording is a series of ticks. Preferably, each call should be logged immediately after its completion, while all details are fresh and clear in the salesman's mind. Calls made by telephone, rather than by visit should not be included, but should be entered on a separate and similar form designed for this purpose.

Another important factor influencing the design of this and other forms is that it should be "fiddle-proof". No salesman should be able to "cook the books" without this fact standing out like a sore thumb when the sales manager analyses the week's results.

All data recorded on the form must be used in the subsequent analysis. If it isn't, don't record it.

The example of the "Call Analysis" form shown in figure A illustrates the method of logging calls. Each call is given a separate line. "Industry Category" denotes the industry to which the particular customer belongs, i.e. Aerospace, Furniture Manufacturer, Steel Stockholder, Supermarkets, whatever the company using the system decides is the most relevant list of industries in their market, or for their products. Code K is normally designated "Miscellaneous" or "Other Industries".

A "No Interview" call is a call where the salesman failed to get past the reception desk. Leaving literature at the desk does not qualify as anything but a "No Interview" call. As the form instructs, if the "No Interview" column is ticked, the relevant columns denoting the type of call it *should* have been, had it been successful, must *also* be ticked.

169

For example, a call on an existing customer, by appointment, to follow up a request from the customer for details on a particular product, but which for unforeseen circumstances found the customer contact suddenly called away on the salesman's arrival, would warrant ticks in the following columns:

No Interview
Call on Existing Customer
Follow up of Lead
Appointment

Calls on potential new customers who have never bought anything from the company before always warrant a tick in the "Call on Prospect" column. A "First Ever Call" is a call where it is the first time ever (to anyone's knowledge) that *anyone* from the company has called on this prospective customer. Obviously, no call will ever have ticks in both "Call on Existing Customer" and "First Ever Call".

The "Follow up of Leads" and "Appointment" columns need no further explanation.

If, during a call, the salesman reaches the stage where a proposal is requested, a tick is warranted in the "Proposal Requested" column, whether the proposal (quotation in many readers' language) is given verbally by the salesman there and then, or whether it will be generated by H.Q. a few days, or weeks later.

If the salesman submits to H.Q. a separate detailed report on any call, a tick is warranted in the "Action Request" column. If he succeeds in securing the actual order or the order number (but not just a verbal promise) a tick goes in the "Order Secured" column.

Any call essentially to rectify or check-out a fault or complaint, where no active selling is done, is usually a "Service Call". Logically, all service calls will be "Calls on Existing Customers".

CALL ANALYSIS

WEEK 14 **SALESMAN** J. WATSON

IF A CALL RESULTS IN "NO INTERVIEW" STILL TICK THE COLUMNS WHICH INDICATE WHAT KIND OF CALL IT SHOULD HAVE BEEN

DATE	COMPANY	Industry Category	No Interview	Call on Existing Customers	Call on Prospect (Pot. New Cust.)	First Ever Call	Follow up of Lead	Appointment	Proposal Requested	Action Request	Order Secured	Service Call	0	1	2	3	4	5	6	7	8	9
M	PRESS STEEL	A	✓					✓					✓									
"	POTTERSBY & CO	B	✓		✓	✓		✓														✓
"	J.B.ENGINEERS	A		✓		✓														✓		
"	HEREFORD & CO	D		✓				✓												✓		
*	EATON & CO	C		✓							✓			✓✓								
T	NYMAN WELDING	B	✓										✓									
"	I.B.E.	D			✓	✓			✓	✓												
"	SMITH DAVIDSON	B	✓		✓	✓			✓	✓												
"	FISHER & MADE	D			✓			✓	✓	✓						✓						
"	AUTOLIFT	B		✓												✓						
"	VICTORIA FORGE	A		✓	✓	✓												✓				
"	ASH & CO	A		✓														✓				
*	BLOGGS & SMALL	D		✓				✓													✓	
*	EXHAUST TOOLS	B		✓				✓	✓				✓			✓						
W	JONES & PLATT	A		✓	✓	✓		✓	✓							✓						
*	BEEDON SMITH	B		✓	✓	✓		✓													✓	
*	DROP FORGES	B			✓	✓			✓												✓	
*	F.LACEY & CO	G			✓	✓		✓	✓							✓						
*	ARUNDEL DEVELOPMENT	D					✓															✓
F	C.K.VALVES	A	✓	✓											✓							
*	BRITISH STEEL	K		✓	✓						✓									✓		
*	AQUASCUTUM	J			✓					✓					✓							
*	WAKEFIELDS	C													✓	✓		✓	✓	✓	✓	✓
	TOTALS		4/15	8	5	9	5	7	3	5	4	0										

	0	1	2	3	4	5	6	7	8	9
INDUSTRY CATEGORY TOTALS	2	1	4	4	1	0	3	2	7	2

BUSINESS MILEAGE 245

A	B	C	D	E	F	G	H	J	K
8	6	2	5	0	0	2	0	1	2

NUMBER OF PROPOSALS SUBMITTED ON PROSPECTS (POT. NEW CUSTOMERS) DURING WEEK: **2**

Figure A. Example of a salesman's call analysis form.

The "Product Need Indentified" section uses another series of prior agreed master codings from the company using the system, as with the A-K Industry Category column. Each product or product group is allocated a number between 0 and 9, and every time the salesman establishes a need for a product or product group on a call, a tick goes in the appropriate column.

At the end of the week, the salesman totals up the ticks in all his columns; totals his calls on the various Industries and fills the totals in at the bottom centre of the form; adds his figure for the total number of proposals or quotations actually submitted to potential new customers (not Existing Customers) during the week (there is another form in the system dealing with "Outstanding Proposals" from which this figure comes and which we will be dealing with later) and sends the "Call Analysis" form off to H.Q., along with his expenses and his "Call Plan" for the next week (another thing we will be discussing later).

The salesman normally retains a copy of his "Call Analysis" form, for future reference and in case the Post Office does something silly with his mail to H.Q. And the following Monday morning, he takes a fresh "Call Analysis" form and the whole process begins again.

What H.Q. does with the Salesman's "Call Analysis" form we shall see in the next chapter.

These kind of "Call Analysis" forms can be tailor-made to suit individual companies where the standard form illustrated does not provide everything the company requires.

Performance Ratios and Analysis

Now on to what H.Q. does with these Call Analysis forms when they arrive on the sales manager's desk on Monday morning.

The sales manager has three functions to perform. First, a cursory check over each Call Analysis form to see how well it related to the Call Plan filed by the salesman for that week—a measure of how well the planning and appointment making worked out in practice.

Second, a mental tally of the number of Action Requests submitted by the salesman during the week (seven on our example) to make sure these were all received and properly actioned, or to verify that the sales manager had in fact seen each Action Request personally, if this is the way he prefers to run his sales operation.

Third, the transfer of the totals on the Call Analysis form to two specially designed record cards which keep steady track of each salesman's personal performance.

Even looking after a dozen salesmen the sales manager should have completed these three operations for all his men, and be into his daily correspondence, by coffee time.

The sales manager has a ring binder for each of his salesmen. Normally, these binders will be kept close at hand, so that the data they contain can be accessed and referred to at any time. This bank of binders is the sales manager's real key to success. Everything he needs to know about his sales operation is within those covers.

Each binder is divided into three sections. In the first section is filed the salesman's Call Plan forms and Call Analysis forms, one of each for each week of the selling year, filed in pairs so that Call Plan and Call Analysis can be viewed together in one double page spread, left to right.

The second section houses the two special records card, that we shall be looking at in detail later in this chapter.

In the third section is filed the salesman's forecast for the whole of the current year, plus any notes the sales manager may have made at the start of the year on expected improvements in the salesman's performance, targets, vices, etc.

Personal Performance Record

Logging the numbers each week that the sales manager receives from his salesmen as totals on the Call Analysis forms, is the easiest and swiftest of the three functions.

The two special performance record cards cover one quarter's sales operation— thirteen weeks of activity. Thus, four sides of the cards make up the whole year.

All the sales manager had to do each Monday is transfer Call Analysis totals for the week in question, to the corresponding columns on the record cards. Fig. A showed week 14 on the Call Analysis form. Follow the figures through to the week 14 lines on the record card illustrations (top line on

173

both). See figs. B and C.

The principle of good performance measurement is to use two main sources of data—the physical activity of the salesman, and his monetary achievements. The data on physical activity comes from the Call Analysis form each week. The data on monetary achievement comes from the H.Q. sales office or accounts department—i.e. total orders received from existing customers and from prospects, and the values of those orders. These figures are logged on the first record card as shown (i.e. 4,824, 1 and 680), the total orders and order value received that week by the company being broken down into the amounts for each individual salesman /territory. Thus, the two main sources of data come together on the one Personal Performance card. Normally, export orders are kept completely separate.

And that's all that needs to be done until the end of the quarter; after, in this case, the figures for week 26 have all been logged.

After the completion of week 26, the figures in each of the columns on the two record cards need to be totalled; on the first card logging the totals in the spaces provided in the "week 26" lines. Thus, the sum total of all the weekly mileage figures for weeks 14 to 26, in the first "mileage" column, is entered in the space to the right of the figure 166—i.e. total mileage 2,660, and so on.

Some totals go on the right of their columns, some on the left, and some both on right *and* left, depending upon what use has to be made of these totals. On the second card, totalling is much simpler.

Provision is made for most of these totals to be compared week by week, in case the company using the system requires a full analysis more frequently than once a quarter. However, experience has found that for most selling situations, analysis once every three months is both adequate and most accurate.

Once the totals have been entered on the first record card, the personal performance ratios for that salesman for that quarter can be computed, simply by taking each pair of totals in turn and dividing the smaller of the two numbers into the larger. Thus J. Watson's miles per call ratio for weeks 14 to 16

174

is 2,660 divided by 288 = 9.2 miles per call.

His abortive call ratio is 288 divided by 44 = 6.5, i.e. for every 6.5 calls made, *one* is abortive.

His calls to order ratio for existing customers is 203 divided by 44 = 4.6, i.e. for every 4.6 calls Watson makes on an existing customer he gets one order. His average order value for repeat business is £13,884 divided by 44 = £315.

The average number of calls he makes on a prospective customer before either writing the prospect off or converting him into a user, is 85 divided by 46 = 1.8 calls.

His calls to proposals submitted ratio on prospects is 85 divided by 33 = 2.6, i.e. for every 2.6 calls made on prospective customers, one proposal, or quotation, is submitted. Following on from this ratio, Watson's proposals to order ratio for prospects is 33 divided by 18 = 1.8, i.e. for every 1.8 proposals submitted, one order is secured. And his average order value for first orders from prospective customers is £4,669 divided by 18 = £259.

Looking at the example of the first record card, it will be seen that J Watson failed to make his New Business target for both the first and the second quarter of that year. Using these last four ratios, the sales manager can quite easily calculate the amounts of extra effort Watson should have put in during weeks 14 to 26, to have *achieved* his New Business target.

To have achieved a New Business target of £5,750 for weeks 14 to 26, at an average order value (achieved) of £259, Watson would have had to secure 5750 divided by 259 = 22 first orders.

He actually achieved 18, so he wasn't far off.

Using the other three ratios, Watson's proposals to orders ratio (achieved) was 1.8, so to get his 22 first orders, he should have submitted 22 x 1.8 = 40 proposals, instead of the 33 he actually did submit.

To submit 40 proposals instead of 33, Watson should have made a total of 40 x 2.6 = 104 calls on prospects instead of 85 calls he *did* make during the quarter. And in respect of the number of new prospects he should have found, researched and called on for the first time that quarter, this should have been 104 divided by 1.8 = 58, instead of the 46 Watson actually found.

PERSONAL PERFORMANCE RECORD
SECOND QUARTER   YEAR 1977   SALESMAN J. WATSON

WEEK	OVERALL					EXISTING CUSTOMERS				
	MILEAGE	MILES PER CALL RATIO CUMULATIVES	TOTAL CALLS	ABORTIVE CALL RATIO CUMULATIVES	NO INTERVIEW	TOTAL CALLS ON USERS	CALLS TO ORDER RATIO CUMULATIVES	TOTAL ORDER RCD FROM USERS	AVERAGE ORDER VALUE REPEAT BUSINESS CUMULATIVES	TOTAL ORDER VALUE FROM USERS
14	245		26		4	18		4		824
15	240		24		5	16		3		716
16	235		25		2	14		5		1016
17	168		20		6	14		1		168
18	196		24		4	17		4		1870
19	247		26		1	15		0		0
20	189		16		3	12		4		1250
21	304		26		5	18		5		1680
22	200		24		4	20		2		420
23	86		10		3	10		0		0
24	240		26		1	19		6		3160
25	175		20		1	15		6		1900
26	166	2660 288	21	288 44	5	15	203 44	4	44 13,884	880
		9.2		65			4.6		315	
				8.0			5.5		296	
				COMPANY NORM			COMPANY NORM		COMPANY NORM	

WEEK	PROSPECTS											
	FIRST EVER CALLS	AVERAGE CALLS ON A PROSPECT CUMULATIVES	TOTAL CALLS ON PROS.	CALLS TO PROPOSALS RATIO CUMULATIVES	PROPOSALS SUBMITTED	PROPOSALS TO ORDER RATIO CUMULATIVES	TOTAL ORDERS RCD FROM PROS. PECTS	AVERAGE ORDER VALUE NEW BUSINESS CUMULATIVES	TOTAL ORDER VALUE FROM PROSPECTS		
14	5		8		2		1		680		
15	3		9		3		2		420		
16	6		11		1		3		1120		
17	6		6		4		2		468		
18	4		7		2		0		0		
19	2		11		3		2		378		
20	2		4		4		1		185		
21	5		8		5		2		410		
22	4		4		1		0		0		
23	0		0		0		0		0		
24	3		7		4		3		526		
25	4		5		2		1		286		
26	2	46 85	6	85 33	2	33 18	1	18 4669	196		
		RATIO Z 1.8		RATIO X 2.6		RATIO Y 1.8		259			
		1.65		2.2		1.75		269			
		COMPANY NORM		COMPANY NORM		COMPANY NORM		COMPANY NORM			

SECOND QUARTER'S REPEAT BUSINESS TARGET

10,500

1st QUARTER DEFICIT

SECOND QUARTER'S NEW BUSINESS TARGET

5,750

1,205   1st QUARTER DEFICIT

Figure B. Example of a salesman's personal performance record card.

A marginal error in performance for most sales organisations, and one which the sales manager can quite easily correct. Watson made his *Repeat* Business target for the quarter comfortably. He also made his repeat business target for the *first* quarter, as no 'deficit' is shown on the card. The company is logically quite happy to take more repeat business than it budgeted for, but the question which the sales manager should put to salesman J Watson is "Could you have still achieved this £13,884 of repeat business with, say, 20 less calls than the 203 calls you actually made on users during weeks 14 to 26?"

The answer will normally be yes. Most salesmen spend a little too much of their time making somewhat ineffective "courtesy" calls on established customers they know well.

So if Watson had spent 20 less calls on existing customers, and devoted these 20 calls to finding and calling on a few more prospects, he would have achieved his New Business target as well as his repeat business target.

A simple re-direction of a small slice of Watson's total effort. Easy to action, once the sales manager knows where to re-direct, and by how much. But without the performance ratios, he would never know.

Watson's performance can be improved yet again by his striving to improve his actual ratios, say, for the New Business part of his activities. Readers will see from the example of the first record card that Watson's ratios are better than the Norm for the company's whole salesforce on *repeat* business, but worse than Norm for the company on *New* Business. How these company norms are calculated we shall discuss at the end of this chapter.

If Watson's personal performance on New Business could be improved so that his own ratios were comparable with the company norm, then for the same number of calls on prospects, (104 for a target achievement for weeks 14 to 26), his actual order value achievement would be:

$$\frac{104 \times 265}{2.2 \times 1.75} = £7,155 \text{ (rounded down)}$$

Taking this calculation step by step, 104 calls at a "calls to proposal" ratio of 2.2 gives 47 proposals submitted. 47 proposals submitted to a "proposals to orders" ratio of 1.75 gives 27 orders. And 27 orders at an average order value of £265 gives £7,155.

What better improvement target for Watson to aim for during the next quarter? Just that very small shift in his ratios, 2.6 to 2.2, 1.8 to 1.75 and £259 to £265. Something highly tangible for him to get his teeth into. And something very easy to achieve. Just marginally more attention paid to the selection and research of new prospects; the relevance to the prospect's own problems of what is said during those critical first minutes of the first call; the accuracy and meaningfulness of the proposals submitted; and the positiveness with which each proposal is followed up and the order asked for.

Even just one selected prospect and proposal per week on which to exert that additional "fluence", and the improvement in performance aimed for is guaranteed.

The second record card, headed "Sales Analysis", fig. C gives the sales manager essential input on how well his salesmen are selling across the whole range of company products, how well they are tackling all the markets for the products in their respective territories, how effective they are at making calls by appointment, and how good the company's back-up is in respect of sales promotion and after sales service.

Looking at salesman J Watson's Sales Analysis card for weeks 14 to 26, we see on the top half of the card the week by week analysis of the products in the company's range for which he established needs with customers or prospects. From the totals of this analysis, it is easy to see that Mr Watson likes talking about product number 8, but dislikes product number 5. Perhaps Watson's territory has few outlets or applications for product 5, and many for product number 8. More likely, however, it is that Watson *believes* in product 8 but doesn't believe sufficiently that product 5 is a sound proposition for his customers.

The sales manager can quite easily check out the extent of potential applications for product 5 in Watson's territory. If potential is good, Watson needs some product training on

178

SALES ANALYSIS — SECOND QUARTER

YEAR _1977_ SALESMAN _J. WATSON_

PRODUCT GROUP ANALYSIS

0	+	1	+	2	+	3	+	4	+	5	+	6	+	7	+	8	+	9	+
2		1		4		5		1				3		2		7		2	
1		4		3		6						2		1		4		3	
3		1		4		7		1		1		3		3		8		4	
1		1		2		3						1		1		6		3	
2		2		2		2		1				3		3		8		2	
3		4		4		5		2		1		3		3		7		5	
2		1		3		3		1		1		2		4		7		4	
1				1		5		2				3		3		6		5	
1		2		3		4		1				2		4		7		5	
		1				2						1		2		3		1	
4		3		3		6		2		2		4		4		6		4	
2		1		2		3		1		1		2		3		5		3	
1		2		1		2						1		3		7		5	
23		**22**		**33**		**53**		**12**		**6**		**30**		**36**		**81**		**46**	

TOTALS

CUSTOMER CATEGORY ANALYSIS

A	B	C	D	E	F	G	H	J	K
8	6	2	5			2		1	2
6	4	3	2	1	2	4		1	1
5	3	4	2	2	3	3	1	1	1
3	2	4	3	1	1	4		2	
4	4	2	4	2	2	4		2	
6	3	4	1	1	1	4	1	3	2
	4	3			2	3	2		2
4	5	2	3	1	1	2	3	2	2
3	4	3	2	2		2	3	5	
1	1	2		1		1		3	1
7	3	2	4	1	1	2	2	4	
1	2	4	3			3	2	5	
3		2	4	2	1	3	2	2	1
51	**41**	**37**	**33**	**14**	**14**	**37**	**17**	**31**	

TOTALS

CALLS ANALYSIS

TOTAL CALLS	BY APP'T	FROM LEAD	SERVICE CALLS
26	11	3	0
24	19	2	1
25	14	4	0
20	10	3	3
24	6	2	0
26	13	2	5
16	12	1	0
26	9	4	0
24	11	3	1
10	4	0	4
26	16	1	0
20	10	3	0
21	9	1	1
288	**144**	**29**	**15**

TOTALS

Figure C. Example of a salesman's sales analysis card.

number 5 to increase his confidence in that section of the company's range.

The product analysis table can also pin-point the salesman who believes in starting his call by opening all his literature and telling the customer about everything his company can supply, irrespective of what the customer actually may want, or the particular problem he may wish the salesman to help solve. This kind of normally ineffective salesman will show abnormally high "product need identified" totals right across the range, most of which are fiction. The problem, once pin-pointed, is equally easy to rectify.

The "Industry Category Analysis" section, bottom left, records Watson's activity in the company's markets; the particular industries where the products are best applied. Just like the product analysis, this industry analysis pin-points areas where the salesman is strong or weak. It also serves to indicate acceptance or rejection of a specific management instruction to the salesforce, say, to concentrate for a month on a particular industry and "push" the products hard in that direction.

The third section, bottom right of the Sales Analysis record card, logs the total calls made by Watson each week, the number made by appointment, the number resulting from leads supplied as a result of the company's sales promotion and advertising activities, and the number of calls made to service products.

The sales manager should be looking for a proportion of calls made by appointment to total calls of no less than 50%. No salesman can make *all* his calls by appointment, but the more he can make, the better. Aim for 60—70% as a sound company norm, depending on the nature of business and the geographical area to be covered.

The "Calls from Lead" column indicates the amount of sales promotional back-up each salesman receives. The more leads the company can supply each salesman the better. Very few salesmen like calling "cold" in their search for new business. But no company that relies on national advertising for lead generation can predict which areas of the country the enquiries will come from. Thus, to maintain a reasonable "spread" of leads across the salesforce, the main national advertising campaign may need to be backed up with more localised mailing campaigns, exhibitions, PR in local newspapers and more advertising in local trade publications.

The "Leads" column enables the sales manager to make sure each and every salesman gets his fair share of leads, and also provides an easy tally of the total effects of the company's sales promotion.

Finally, the "Service Calls" column gives an indication to the sales manager of when his salesmen are starting to spend too much of their time doing the job the service department should be doing. The figures can determine when additional service staff should be employed, and in which territories. In the case of salesman Watson, the time he spent on his fifteen service calls during weeks 14 to 26 might have more fruitfully been devoted to the achievement of that New Business target. One more arrow to the sales manager's bow.

Company Norms

Now for those company norms that somehow found themselves on Watson's personal performance record card.

The sales manager, apart from a ring binder for each of his salesmen, also has one for himself. In his "Master Record" binder, he keeps the quarterly totals from his salesmen's record cards, and computes the Norms for the company's overall performance.

The SCRS system provides him with a set of three Master Record cards on which his figures are logged for each quarter. The first master card computes the performance norms for the salesforce, the second consolidates the information on products, industries, appointments, leads and service calls recorded on the salesmen's Sales Analysis cards, and the third totals the salesmen's individual sales forecasts for the year in question and breaks the forecasts down into product groups so that the sales manager has the most meaningful data to feed to his production departments to guide the company's manufacturing effort. This third master card will be discussed in detail in a later chapter which will cover sales forecasting.

Each of the two MASTER cards illustrated in Figures D and E has provision for 25 salesmen, a substantial salesforce for most companies. For situations involving *more* than 25 salesmen, either a special set of MASTER record cards can be designed to suit, or two cards can be used, on a "carried forward—brought forward" basis, or the norms can be produced on a regional basis if the company operates with regional sales managers.

Looking more closely at the figures on the "Activity Analysis" second master card, a few more observations can be made. For example, the totals for the Product Groups, bottom left, indicates that products 8, 3, 9 and 7 are the most popular, and in that order. This fact can be checked against the year's sales forecast and the company's product life cycle predictions for the product range, to make sure forecasts and predictions are still up to date. Similarly, the Industry Category totals can pin-point a particular industry or market application that is waxing or waning, and so guide the sales manager in his decision as to what to do to rectify the deviation, if rectified the problem can be. If not, plans should be changed accordingly.

And as a footnote, if anyone is wondering what the "Miles per Call" ratio on the Personal Performance record card doesn't have a Company Norm, it is because this particular ratio cannot be averaged out. The salesman selling in the heart of London, or the Black Country, will have a totally different "Miles per Call" ratio to the salesman who sells in Devon and Cornwall. This ratio is thus kept individual, and the sales manager simply aims at keeping each salesman's figures as *low* as possible.

Summing up on this Chapter

If a salesman is above or below his target, then his sales manager needs to be able to measure *WHY*. This pre-supposes of course that the target itself is accurately set.

The SCRS system measures a salesman's effectiveness based on the logical steps of any selling process, as advocated by Structured Training Limited on its courses for salesmen and sales managers. These steps never vary, except in respect of Demonstrations, which in cases of capital equipment selling normally takes place *AFTER* the proposal is submitted, but *CAN* take place at any point from the Approach onwards, or be omitted altogether.

SALESMAN	TOTAL CALLS	NO INTER-VIEWS	CALLS ON USERS	ORDERS FROM USERS	TOTAL ORDER VALUE FROM USERS	FIRST EVER CALLS	CALLS ON PROSPTS	PROP'LS SUB-MITTED	ORDERS FROM PROSPTS	TOTAL ORDER VALUE FROM PROSPECTS
J. Watson	205	44	203	44	13 884	46	85	33	18	4,669
R. Briggs	264	32	168	27	8,903	51	96	44	27	6,463
L. Sotton	249	28	202	31	9.275	36	47	11	8	2,761
F. White	296	31	175	27	8,740	68	121	57	31	7,892
G. Hope	321	43	212	41	8,202	59	109	49	28	6,720
A Rolfe	199	37	142	20	7,966	29	57	19	14	7,995
B. Stein	255	42	170	26	8,449	56	85	39	22	5,977
S. Arm	253	30	166	32	9,791	66	87	48	24	6,502
J. Jones	241	21	175	31	9,464	41	66	35	20	4,744
W. Ask	302	26	204	52	13,242	64	98	52	29	8,842
TOTALS	2,268	X	1,817	331	97,976	516	851	387	221	58,565

COMPANY NORMS PERIOD *SECOND QUARTER WEEKS 14-26*

Abortive call Ratio	$\frac{A\ 2668}{B\ 334}$	8.0 to 1	Average calls on a Prospect	$\frac{G\ 851}{F\ 516}$	1.65
Calls to orders Ratio (Users)	$\frac{C\ 1817}{D\ 331}$	5.5 to 1	Calls to proposals Ratio (Prospects)	$\frac{G\ 851}{H\ 387}$	2.2 to 1
Average order Value (Users)	$\frac{E\ 97976}{D\ 331}$	£296	Proposals to orders Ratio (Prospects)	$\frac{H\ 387}{221}$	1.75 to 1
			Average order Value (Prospects)	$\frac{K\ 58565}{J\ 221}$	£265

Figure D. Example of a company performance norms card.

ACTIVITY ANALYSIS PERIOD SECOND QUARTER WEEKS 14 to 26

SALESMAN	PRODUCT GROUP TOTALS										INDUSTRY CATEGORY TOTALS										TOTAL CALLS	TOTAL APPOINT- MENT	% of Total	TOTAL FROM LEADS	% of Total	TOTAL SERVICE CALLS	% of Total
	0	1	2	3	4	5	6	7	8	9	A	B	C	D	E	F	G	H	J	K							
J WATFORD	23	41	33	52	12	6	30	59	81	46	51	41	37	32	14	14	37	17	31	13	2285	1444	50	29	10	51	5.2
R BEARS	16	26	27	57	141	41	41	47	42	94	55	40	55	45	11	4	41	21	31	9	244	102	73	26	10	17	6.4
L POTTON	161	41	53	101	55	66	26	66	49	84	42	86	33	61	10	9	21	4	41	9	249	103	41	13	5	7	3.4
F WINTERS	24	81	44	24	13	31	81	58	83	25	68	13	42	47	8	44	6	11	31	12	296	244	58	81	9	41	4.9
G HOKINS	29	21	24	44	11	4	17	4	99	15	24	76	24	15	13	11	53	41	31	16	324	272	95	24	11	24	5.2
A ROFE	36	41	20	42	12	17	22	44	45	41	82	51	42	18	4	2	14	4	44	12	199	140	70	44	21	44	7.0
D SUEN	19	27	29	52	81	6	22	44	40	47	05	56	22	22	4	17	38	4	21	4	255	142	50	47	11	7	2.7
S DORES	20	19	28	59	89	39	24	41	72	44	44	30	26	10	7	45	4	17	25	12	252	127	65	81	7	21	8.2
J JONES	24	21	20	61	14	24	24	44	77	52	54	31	26	41	41	7	84	23	41	42	167	101	44	24	10	41	6.8
W HORGON	27	31	23	44	12	21	52	24	41	48	71	53	44	44	28	4	40	41	21	3	206	552	66	24	41	8	9.2
TOTALS	235	252	253	142	22	5	135	413	437	447	155	366	151	274	338	154	257	267			2669	1858	101	272	01	121	1.5

Figure E. Example of a sales force activity analysis card.

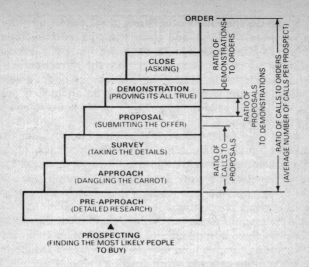

ORDER

| CLOSE (ASKING) |
| DEMONSTRATION (PROVING ITS ALL TRUE) |
| PROPOSAL (SUBMITTING THE OFFER) |
| SURVEY (TAKING THE DETAILS) |
| APPROACH (DANGLING THE CARROT) |
| PRE-APPROACH (DETAILED RESEARCH) |

▲

PROSPECTING
(FINDING THE MOST LIKELY PEOPLE TO BUY)

RATIO OF DEMONSTRATIONS TO ORDERS

RATIO OF PROPOSALS TO DEMONSTRATIONS

RATIO OF CALLS TO PROPOSALS

RATIO OF CALLS TO ORDERS
(AVERAGE NUMBER OF CALLS PER PROSPECT)

The steps of the selling process, and some of the ratios produced by the SCRS system

Predicting and Avoiding Catastrophes

IF ONE OF YOUR BEST salesmen left you next month for pastures new, how much would this reduce your turnover, and how long would it take to recruit a replacement and train him up to full effectiveness?

If you've no performance ratios and norms to work from, you're going to have a hard time with this calculation. It isn't simply a reduction equal to the lost salesman's last year's business.

Once he has his performance ratios and company norms, the sales manager can use them to check out the likely result of taking quite a number of different kinds of action—before he pushes any buttons. Thus, many a wrong move can be avoided without anyone knowing.

For example:

How would a couple of additional salesmen in the North West change the picture? How long would it take to cover their costs?

What would be the effect of splitting the London territory, which is currently vacant, and giving half to Fred Johnson in Croydon and half to George Davies in Watford? Will a move like this get us more business, or reduce the effectiveness of these salesmen in the territories they are responsible for now?

How would turnover and profitability be affected if product X was taken out of the range? How would new product Y change the status quo?

If our average order value could be increased, by changing the style of packaging, or the range of accessories, or by offering incentives for minimum quantities, how would this affect the salesforce's work load if total turnover were to remain the same? And how would a reduction in the average order value affect the position?

If we reduced the number of salesmen and spent the money they cost on more advertising and sales promotion to provide leads for the salesmen whom we retain, how would this better or worsen our turnover and profit position?

All these questions, and many more, can be answered accurately by using the ratios and norms produced by the kind of system we have been discussing.

The Total Package

ANY SALES MANAGER reading this extract will be sure by now that changing the habits of a lifetime and implementing a salesforce control system like SCRS is not going to be easy. Absolutely right.

From the date of implementation, it will be at least six months before all the hang-ups, misunderstandings, obstructions, negative attitudes and straight lead swinging are ironed out, and the sales manager can be really confident that he has emerged as a leader of men from his "one of the boys" position, commands much more respect from his sales team and from above, and that his figures and projections are accurate and present a sound basis on which his company can build for the future.

Once this has been achieved, the team effort will be unbeatable.

SCRS is expensive, probably the *MOST* expensive salesforce

control system available as a standard package, because it gives a company much more than paperwork, binders and boxes. SCRS executives are themselves management consultants. Every time the system is sold, the company purchasing it gets up to two days management consultancy and training; half a day at the initial meeting with the company's directors, when all the selling problems are out on the table and most of them resolved; half a day when the system is introduced to the company's salesforce, when other selling problems from the "sharp end" are normally resolved and any initial resentment by the salesforce to a new system is dissipated by the SCRS executive himself; half a day three months later, to make sure the first quarter's results are being properly produced and to guide the sales manager in what corrective action and training he should undertake with specific salesmen, based on these results; and finally, if necessary, half a day at the end of the second quarter's operation of the SCRS system, as a final check to make sure everything is going according to plan.

The guarantee a company gets with SCRS is unconditional. If the system is sold to a company, it is right for that company. If, subsequently, the company experiences problems, SCRS executives will resolve all these problems, make changes to the system if necessary, counsel members of the company's staff, spend time in the field with salesmen —whatever is necessary to have the system operating effectively and giving the company what it set out to achieve.

SCRS does not have unhappy customers. This is a dictum which is religiously adhered to. The reputation so generated is far too valuable ever to be abused or neglected.

A proportion of the price a company pays for the SCRS system goes, of course, to cover the very high costs of the system's development since 1966, development which still continues.

The final factor which makes SCRS the most *effective* system available is its presentation. The system is designed to *LOOK* professional, as well as *BE* professional. This is important because salesmen the world over tend to be the leading experts at abusing things. And this fact, coupled with their

187

inherent hatred of paperwork of any kind, would tend to destroy SCRS before it even got started, were the system to be cheaply presented.

So boxes are top quality marine plywood, covered in black grained leather-cloth. Ring binders are padded and gold blocked. Manilla files and cards are extra heavy grade, not light grade. More than enough forms are supplied rather than just enough. The entire presentation and packaging of the system is designed for the salesman's respect—and with respect comes proper use.

This extract covers but one section of the SCRS salesforce control system—Performance Measurement. Other sections not mentioned here cover Customer Records, Prospecting, Planning Ahead, Sales Forecasting and Keeping track on Best Bets. All these sections are fully detailed in the complete SCRS manual.

27–SALES FORCE CONTROL

Your personal estimate of the percentage improvement possible.

Prices	Variable Costs
Sales (10%)	Fixed Costs

The figure in brackets is our management consultant's estimate of the average percentage improvement gained in the first year by a business successfully implementing the SCRS system.

Use this space for notes, calculations and for drafting your letter to SCRS requesting the manual or a visit. The address is:

Sales Control & Record Systems Limited
Concorde House
24 Warwick New Road
Royal Leamington Spa
Warwickshire CV32 5JH
Telephone: 0926 37621-4
Telex: 311746

28–DO YOU KNOW ANYONE ELSE............?

Our management consultant spent a few days out with our salesmen, observing how they went about selling. Generally he says they were pretty good, but on one point, he says they slip up every time.

Now I know what this point is; it gives me hysterics, because it is so bloody simple—and if we can rectify the error it could not only boost our sales, it could also save us a lot of money on unnecessary advertising.

The point occurs at the end of each and every call our salesmen make. They shut their brief cases, re-confirm arrangements for the next call on the particular customer they are with (a good point) and then say good-bye.

Thus, I am told (and fully agree), they throw away a golden opportunity to fish for new contacts on every call they make.

What they should be asking, just after the re-confirmation of the next call and **before** saying good-bye, is:-

"By the way, before I go, do you know anyone else in this area who could use UWC products......? or *"Who could use our kind of equipment.......?*

or—for regular clients—*"I know I've asked you this before, George, but just in case, is there anyone worth me calling on, this time around.......?*

or—for very large companies with lots of departments—*"By the way, before I go, are there any other departments here that could use our kind of equipment......?*

The range of possibilities for this kind of question are practically endless, but whatever variety fits, the salesman stands to get either a positive or a negative reply.

If negative, he simply says *"Ah well, hope you didn't mind me asking,"* and says good-bye in the usual way.

But if the reply is **positive**—a name—whether a name the salesman knows, or doesn't know; whether an existing customer or not, the opportunity is there to ask more questions—

with absolutely no fear of being stopped.

"What do they do....?

"What kind of widgets do they use at present...?

"Have they any problems....?

"Who's your opposite number over there.....?

"Do you know him well...?

"I wonder, would you mind if I mentioned your name when I telephone for an appointment...?

It's so simple. And so certain of success. Every time the salesman gets a positive response to his first question, he finishes up with a fully qualified, fully researched prospective customer, and with a third party reference to mention when he telephones the prospective customer.

So why do we do so much advertising to generate enquiries for our salesmen to follow up? If they asked the appropriate question at the end of every call they made, they would generate for themselves more than enough prospects to fill the time they have available for New Business selling. And the prospects they generate would probably be better than the ones we get from our advertising, to boot.

This task is so absurdly easy that I can envisage some of our salesmen going even further with certain customers. After the question:

"Do you know him well.....?

if the response has been *"Yes, we play golf together every week"* or something like that—the salesman's final question might be:

"I wonder, would you mind giving Mr Brown a ring for me now, to find out if he could see me this afternoon, while I'm in this area....?

I'm told that most customers asked to do this, do it— and do it quite happily. Thinking about it, I would do it too, if a salesman asked me properly.

So let's get all our salesmen working this way. Get the necessary instructions out fast. Prepare scripts like this to be certain they all know what to do, and how to do it.

There is only one logical reason (or excuse) why salesmen don't ask questions like these on every call they make—after they know what to do—**THEY FORGET.**

I'll personally fire any salesman who forgets something this important—and his manager with him.

Timing Appointments

Here is another little gem which follows on from "Do you know anyone else....?

The Salesmen in most of our divisions have problems making enough appointments, yet they all know that it is much easier to do business on an appointment call than on a "cold" call.

I have been told of a piece of basic psychology which might help boost the number of appointments secured, and therefore the amount of business subsequently secured:-

Customers who are telephoned by salesmen normally have an inbuilt resistance to the salesman. They are also busy people who don't have enough time as it is. So they don't feel very pleased about the idea of giving up some of their time to see salesmen unless it is critically important to **them**.

90% of salesmen plan their work and their time hour by hour—and **on** the hour. Thus, when they telephone a customer or a potential customer for an appointment, they say *"How about 10.00 am?"* or *"Can I call to see you at 3 pm?"*

The customers who hear this, subconsciously say to themselves *"This salesman will keep me an hour"*, and as an hour is a large chunk of their day, the majority will decline to see the salesman.

9% of salesmen plan more meticulously and can therefore call at other times than just "on the hour". They often say to their customers and potential customers, *"How about 10.30 am?"* or *"Can I call to see you at 3.30 pm?"*

These customer say to themselves *"This salesman will keep me half an hour,"*. and so, this 9% of salesmen get a better success rate than the 90% of salesmen who only suggest "on the hour" times.

But the salesmen who win most of the time are the 1% who have learned the psychology of the situation and use this to positive effect. They suggest to their customers and potential customers times like 8.50 am, 9.50 am, 10.50 am, 11.50 am, 2.50 pm, 4.50 pm etc.

Not only does this indicate to most customers that the

salesman is a highly professional planner, it also leads most customers to feel that **this** salesman will only take up **ten minutes** of valuable time.

So make sure all your salesmen are fully aware of this.

28—DO YOU KNOW ANYONE ELSE?

Your personal estimate of the percentage improvement possible.

Prices	Variable Costs
Sales	Fixed Costs
(10%)	(2%)

The figures in brackets are our management consultant's estimate of the probable percentage improvement in a business where the sales force does a lot of "cold canvas" calling on a wide range of industries.

Use this space for notes and calculations.

29–WHEN BUSINESS IS SLACK

Send out a questionnaire to find out what the customers think of us.

The answers we get to this kind of questionnaire would pinpoint ways in which we are going wrong and could thus improve our business. Returned Questionnaires will normally give our salesmen the opportunity of a prompt follow-up, and this will mean more business and higher morale. Our customers will feel we care more about them than most of their suppliers.

Here is an example used by a wholesaler to test his retail customers. Use it as a guide for when you produce your own questionnaires.

1. How often does our salesman call? ☐ too frequently ☐ not enough ☐ just right	4. Do our orders take about as long to deliver as those of other wholesalers? ☐ as long ☐ longer ☐ shorter
2. Does he come at the right time of day? ☐ Yes ☐ No If no, he should come: ☐ in the morning ☐ at mid-day ☐ in the afternoon ☐ in the evening	5. When you telephone us do you get the information you require? ☐ quickly or do you sometimes ☐ have to wait
3. Does he know his stuff? ☐ very well ☐ adequately ☐ inadequately	6. Is the range we offer you? ☐ too small ☐ just right ☐ too large? If too small, what else should we offer you?

7. How important to you are our services in the following area?	very important	interesting	not so important
a) Display	☐	☐	☐
b) Regular visits from salesmen	☐	☐	☐
c) Fast delivery	☐	☐	☐
d) Expert advice on our premises	☐	☐	☐
e) Loan of equipment	☐	☐	☐
f) Advertising support	☐	☐	☐
g) Good warehouse selection	☐	☐	☐
h) Aids to calculation	☐	☐	☐
i) Credit terms	☐	☐	☐
j) Sales promotion	☐	☐	☐
k) Special offers/campaigns	☐	☐	☐
l) Price structure right for the market	☐	☐	☐

Example reproduced by courtesy of Leviathan House Ltd.

29—WHEN BUSINESS IS SLACK

Your personal estimate of the percentage improvement possible.

Prices	Variable Costs
Sales (5%)	**Fixed Costs**

The figure in brackets is our management consultant's estimate of the probable percentage improvement in a business which has a lot of regular customers in a highly competitive market.

Use this space for notes and calculations.

What is a Customer?

A Customer is the most important person in this Firm . . . . whether he comes in person, writes to us or telephones.

A Customer is not dependent upon us . . . we depend upon him for our living.

A Customer is not an interruption of our work. . . .he is the purpose of it. He is doing us a favour by giving us the opportunity to serve him.

A Customer is not someone with whom to argue or match our wits. No one ever won an argument with a customer.

A Customer is a person who comes to us because he needs certain goods or services. It is our job to provide them in a way profitable to him and to ourselves.

A Customer is not a cold statistic . . . he is a flesh and blood human being with emotions and prejudices like our own.

A Customer is the most important person in this Firm . . . without him there would be no business.

30–PACKAGING

On a quick count, seventeen of our products, all "consumable" powders and liquids, are packed in round containers—or cylindrical to be more accurate.

Did it occur to anyone (it didn't to me until it was pointed out by that fast becoming insufferable management consultant of ours) that if we could change those seventeen containers to a square—or more accurately rectangular shape, without increasing their overall dimensions, we would increase their volume by 27½%.

With customers who buy by the container, or by the dozen or hundred containers, this could mean an increase in sales of 27½%, because although the price per container will go up, and be accepted by customers because they see they are getting 27½% more product, they are not likely to buy many less containers, or re-sell many less containers on the retail side of our business.

There are other benefits, both to us and our retailer customers. Square containers are easier to pack than round ones. More stable. So we can save money on our physical distribution costs. Likewise square containers are easier to stack and display on customers' shelves or in their stores. And the label on a square container is about 30% more visible than on a round container, getting the message across better both for us and our customers.

Remembering the old joke about the twist drill manufacturer who decided to go metric but still sold his metric sized drills by the dozen, we also seem to have some mileage to gain in paying closer attention to the quantities we sell. Are our "pack" sizes right for maximum volume? If we increase the quantity of items per pack for some of our small 'bit' products, could we increase our sales just like that? Our management consultant reckons that for some of our 'bit' products that are sold by the pack, a change of quantity could boost sales by up to 20%.

On our capital equipment products, are we paying enough attention to the eye appeal of our products? Do we take them for granted? If they **looked** more attractive would we sell more; would our salesmen **like** selling them more?

Would a change of colour do anything to enhance the image of the product; the projection of its inferred quality to the customer? We have a few yellow and red products. Would they look better if they were two-tone grey/blue or beige and brown, the 'quality' colours? It wouldn't cost us much to try it and find out.

Do any of our products need a face lift? Cosmetic surgery it's called. Round off square corners, streamline cowlings, modernise grills, chemical black instead of chrome plate. That kind of thing.

In the Hi-Fi market, the military kind of design seems to be all the rage. My wife calls it "army issue"; but it obviously sells. Are we sufficiently fashion conscious with our lumps of machinery and equipment?

So here are the first three areas in packaging:-

the shape of containers

the quantity per pack

the eye appeal of the product

Every division in UWC can improve things in at least one of these three areas and increase sales as a result. There may well be quite a few more areas over and above these three, so keep looking.

30–PACKAGING
Your personal estimate of the percentage improvement possible.

Prices	Variable Costs
Sales (10%)	Fixed Costs

The figure in brackets is our management consultant's estimate of the probable percentage improvement in a business where packaging is predominately cylindrical and some of it could be changed to rectangular, and where pack quantities provide some scope for change.

Use this space for notes and calculations.

YOUR FINAL CALCULATIONS

Well, that's all the treatment areas I'm covering for our first year of action. Now what you have to do is backtrack through this Action Plan and add up the personal estimates you have made at the end of each treatment area.

When you have the totals, enter them in the box below.

(If you are confident that you know of any other treatment areas in your bit of our business which would warrant immediate attention, then by all means make notes for circulation at next month's meeting and add your estimates for these additional areas to your totals).

Total Personal Estimates

PRICES_____%   **VARIABLE COSTS**_____%

SALES_____%   **FIXED COSTS**_____%

Finally, use your totals on the sheet following and see how much **BETTER** than Double you are capable of achieving.

Work down the boxes doing the same compound calculations you did at the beginning, but this time using **YOUR** figures. If **your** bit of the business has different 'Starting Situation' figures, change these to yours.

Manufacturing

1 STARTING SITUATION

SALES	VARIABLE COSTS (Costs of making the stuff)	
100		**50**
	FIXED COSTS (Overheads)	**40**
	GM	**10**

2 COSTS reduced by

SALES	VARIABLE COSTS	%
	FIXED COSTS	%
		%
	GM	

3 PRICES raised by   %

SALES	VARIABLE COSTS	
	FIXED COSTS	
	GM	

4 SALES increased by %

SALES	VARIABLE COSTS	
	FIXED COSTS	
	GM	

Distribution

1 STARTING SITUATION

SALES	VARIABLE COSTS (Costs of buying the stuff)	
100		**70**
	FIXED COSTS (Overheads)	**20**
	GM	**10**

2 COSTS reduced by

SALES	VARIABLE COSTS	%
	FIXED COSTS	%
		%
	GM	

3 PRICES raised by   %

SALES	VARIABLE COSTS	
	FIXED COSTS	
	GM	

4 SALES increased by %

SALES	VARIABLE COSTS	
	FIXED COSTS	
	GM	

RECOMMENDED READING

Our management consultant has written two books on industrial selling and sales management, which are well worth your reading. These are *The A—Z of Industrial Salesmanship* (published by William Heinemann) and *The A—Z of Sales Management* (published by Pan Books).

Another book worth acquiring to help you achieve your own "Double Profits" target is *Managing for Results* by Peter F. Drucker (also published by Pan Books).

One of your greatest problems will be to find the time to do something about all the treatment areas in this Action Plan.

Here is an extract from *The A—Z of Sales Management* which aptly spells out the answer to this problem:-

"Blue Assed Fly Disease"

Do you love working in a panic situation?

Many Managers do. Maybe it's a question of adrenalin flow. Everything is left to the last minute. Everyone in the department has to work overtime. The deadline is met, but only after everyone's lost a couple of pounds in sweat.

Only the manager who suffers from B.A.F. disease gets any feeling of satisfaction for a job well done, if the job was done that way. His staff reckon he's a pain. Inconsiderate and irresponsible. And when you get down to brass tacks, it only happens because of a lack of selfdiscipline, leading to a lack of planning.

Remember the old office joke, hanging on the wall......
'If you can keep your head while everyone round is losing theirs—it means you haven't the slightest idea what's going on'.

...... Well, the good manager works to the opposite of this. He keeps his head **and** knows the score. He sets an example and calms everyone down. He has learned the secret of planning. Start at the point in time when the job has to be completed—and work **back** towards now. Not the other way round. From the time plan, establish what has to be done, who has to do it, and delegate each task clearly, building in deadlines for each delegated action. Then relax and have it all happen, being available to mop up any hang-ups or unforeseen problems.

Using Your Time More Profitably

A number of business surveys have indicated that the average manager works fifty to sixty hours a week. He takes home with him and lives with a wife who struggles, often unsuccessfully, to keep him human.

He carries his work, often unfinished, back to the office. There he will have one hour alone each day, being interrupted every eight minutes by subordinates or other executives seeking advice or answers to problems. Most of these problems are things other employees are being paid to resolve.

He spends 80% of his time communicating and only 20% doing creative work (which includes THINKING.)

The Chest and Heart Association say this is fatal.

So set yourself some objectives:

1. *To reduce interruptions by 50%.*
2. *To reduce time spent on the telephone by 50%.*
3. *To reduce time spent on correspondence by 30%.*
4. *To double the time spent on planning and thinking.*
5. *To allow half-an-hour every day for self-analysis and creativity.*
6. *To delegate properly a further 20% of your own workload.*
7. *To make full use of your secretary.*

If you need to start by analysing what you do at present, get your secretary to list everything that happens for a full week. It will frighten you to death.

Costings

If your working year contains 238 days, your salary is £10,000 p.a. and the company's overheads are 200%, your time is costing this:

1 minute	£ 0.30
5 minutes	£ 1.50
10 minutes	£ 3.00

30 minutes	£ 9.00
1 hour	£ 18.00
1 day	£126.00

This doesn't include your car and expenses.

It was Peter Drucker (Managing for Results) who said:
"The greatest single cause of executive inefficiency is **Overwork**".

It was Robert Townsend (Avis Rent-a-Car) who said:
"If you've got a guy who's good in a crisis, get rid of him, or you'll always have one".

POSTSCRIPT

Finally, here's a personal message from me to all of you.

Everything in this Action Plan is just plain common sense. That's pretty obvious.

What is also obvious is that quite a few people in the organisation are going to have to change their ways of doing the job, their attitudes towards the business, quite a bit.

That's life. Change is what brings progress. The ability to accept and work happily and efficiently with change is what separates the men from the boys.

So bear this in mind. I am personally dedicated to seeing the whole of this Action Plan successfully implemented within the year. The benefits of doing this, for all of us, are beyond doubt, and considerable.

Remembering the old motto "If you're not part of the Solution, you've got to be part of the Problem", take serious note therefore—anyone who puts obstacles in the way of our progress is going to get flattened.

Let's get to work.

Group Managing Director,
Universal Widget Corporation.

The only alternative to perseverance is failure.

Alastair Mant

The Rise and Fall of the British Manager

£1.20

'Seeks to explain, in a vigorous style, why in this country we
"downgrade so many of the jobs that really matter" ... Mant argues
that the business of making and selling things, and doing these jobs
well, has been submerged by the preoccupation with "management", as if it was something quite distinct from these humdrum
activities' FINANCIAL TIMES

'What ails the British economy, he claims, is not the quality of its
management, but the fact that management exists at all' NEW
STATESMAN

'Managers and management teachers who are anxious to
explore new and more effective means of improving management
performance will not be deterred'
MANAGEMENT REVIEW AND DIGEST

C. Northcote Parkinson and
Nigel Rowe

Communicate £1.20

Parkinson's formula for business survival. Peter Drucker says in his
Foreword: 'This book, to my knowledge for the first time, tackles all
four elements of communication (what to say; when to say it; whom
to say it to; how to say it). It makes the businessman literate and it
gives him the competence which he needs.'

'Will be read avidly by the professionals and the amateurs in PR, but
it is the individual businessman who will gain most from it'
DIRECTOR

Desmond Goch
Finance and Accounts for Managers £1.25

The art of accountancy is now the most important instrument of control in the management armoury. This comprehensive guide will enable managers — even those without formal training in business finance — to formulate trading policies, forecast future trends and effectively administer their departments.

Rosemary Stewart
The Reality of Organizations £1.25

'Addressed to managers whether in industry, commerce, hospitals, public administration or elsewhere and includes examples from these latter fields ... its style is excellent, concise and free of jargon' PUBLIC ADMINISTRATION

The Reality of Management £1.25

'Not just another manual for executives, it is rather more like a set of compass bearings to help the manager plot his course in his career and his social life' NEW SOCIETY

Margaret Hennig and Anne Jardim
The Managerial Woman £1.20

'Practical suggestions for women who are setting out on the climb to the top' FINANCIAL TIMES

'Why do so many women founder on the lowly rungs of the executive ladder? *The Managerial Woman* attempts to provide an answer by telling ambitious women how to overcome the worst pitfalls' DAILY MAIL

'For this book 3,000 women were involved in seminars or interviews and twenty-five who had made it were interviewed in great depth' DIRECTOR

R. E. Palmer and A. H. Taylor

Financial Planning for Managers £1.75

Today, more than ever before, it is essential that management has a sound appreciation of the financial implications of its plans and actions. Using clear, everyday language the authors explain the nature of the assistance which higher levels of accounting can provide in the planning and control of a modern business.

'It really is excellent value and offers an intensely practical approach' CERTIFIED ACCOUNTANTS JOURNAL

Peter F. Drucker

Management £2.50

Peter Drucker's aim in this major book is 'to prepare today's and tomorrow's managers for performance'. He presents his philosophy of management, refined as a craft with specific skills: decision making, communication, control and measurement, analysis — skills essential for effective and responsible management in the late twentieth century.

'Crisp, often arresting ... A host of stories and case histories from Sears Roebuck, Marks and Spencer, IBM, Siemens, Mitsubishi and other modern giants lend colour and credibility to the points he makes' ECONOMIST

Peter F. Drucker
The Practice of Management £1.95

'Peter Drucker has three outstanding gifts as a writer on business –
acute perception, brilliant skill as a reporter and unlimited self-
confidence ... his penetrating accounts of the Ford Company ...
Sears Roebuck ... IBM ... are worth a library of formal business
histories' NEW STATESMAN

'Those who now manage ought to read it: those who try to teach
management ought to buy it'
TIMES EDUCATIONAL SUPPLEMENT

Managing for Results 95p

'A guide to do-it-yourself management ... contains first-class
suggestions that have the great virtue that they are likely to be
widely and easily applicable to almost every business'
TIMES REVIEW OF INDUSTRY

The Effective Executive £1.25

'A specific and practical book about how to be an executive who
contributes ... The purpose of this book is to induce the executive to
concentrate on his own contribution and performance, with his
attention directed to improving the organization by serving outsiders
better. I believe Mr Drucker achieves this purpose simply and
brilliantly – and in the course of doing so offers many insights into
executive work and suggestions for improving executive performance. I can conscientiously recommend that this book be given the
very highest priority for executive reading and even rereading'
DIRECTOR

Reference, language and information

☐ **Pan Dictionary of Synonyms and Antonyms**		£1.95p
☐ **Travellers' Multilingual Phrasebook**		£1.95p
☐ **Universal Encyclopaedia of Mathematics**		£2.95p

Literature guides

☐ **An Introduction to Shakespeare and his Contemporaries**	Marguerite Alexander	£2.95p
☐ **An Introduction to Fifty American Poets**	Peter Jones	£1.75p
☐ **An Introduction to Fifty Modern British Plays**	Benedict Nightingale	£2.95p
☐ **An Introduction to Fifty American Novels**	Ian Ousby	£1.95p
☐ **An Introduction to Fifty British Novels 1600—1900**	Gilbert Phelps	£2.50p
☐ **An Introduction to Fifty Modern European Poets**	John Pilling	£2.95p
☐ **An Introduction fo Fifty British Poets 1300—1900**	Michael Schmidt	£1.95p
☐ **An Introduction to Fifty Modern British Poets**		£2.95p
☐ **An Introduction to Fifty European Novels**	Martin Seymour-Smith	£1.95p
☐ **An Introduction to Fifty British Plays 1660—1900**	John Cargill Thompson	£1.95p

All these books are available at your local bookshop or newsagent, or can be ordered direct from the publisher. Indicate the number of copies required and fill in the form below

9

....

Name_____
(Block letters please)

Address_____

_____

Send to Pan Books (CS Department), Cavaye Place, London SW10 9PG
Please enclose remittance to the value of the cover price plus:
35p for the first book plus 15p per copy for each additional book ordered
to a maximum charge of £1.25 to cover postage and packing
Applicable only in the UK

While every effort is made to keep prices low, it is sometimes
necessary to increase prices at short notice. Pan Books reserve
the right to show on covers and charge new retail prices which
may differ from those advertised in the text or elsewhere